100 Little Reading Comprehension Lessons

Fun-to-read stories with skill-building exercises

Written by Margaret Brinton

Illustrated by Len Shalansky

Teaching & Learning Company

1204 Buchanan St., P.O. Box 10
Carthage, IL 62321-0010

This book belongs to

Cover design by Sara King

Copyright © 2004, Teaching & Learning Company
ISBN No. 978-1-57310-425-8
ISBN No. 1-57310-425-6

Printing No. 9876543

Teaching & Learning Company
1204 Buchanan St., P.O. Box 10
Carthage, IL 62321-0010

Table of Contents

Dear Teacher or Parent,

It was a wonderful privilege for me to be able to create *100 Little Reading Comprehension Lessons* for your students. I used fiction for some of the lessons with the intention of delighting and entertaining your students, and I used non-fiction for other lessons with the hope of expanding their knowledge and awareness.

While the comprehension questions are an important aspect of each lesson, it is the actual content of each reading passage that I hope you will make full use of. As the teacher or parent, I suggest that you read each lesson aloud to the children prior to their seeing the page. Doing so will expand their auditory senses and awaken them to the pleasure of each story. Following the oral reading, I suggest that you distribute the page to the children and allow them to read the story silently and attack the comprehension questions. Finally, each session can be completed with an oral re-reading of the story and a review of the comprehension activity.

Reading is an adventure! Embark on it!

Sincerely,

Margaret

Margaret Brinton

Little Hedgehog

A hedgehog is a small animal. It is covered with rough hair and sharp spines. To protect itself from a fox, it rolls up into a ball. The pointy spines stick out all over it. Now the fox cannot eat the hedgehog!

A hedgehog likes to have a lot of space. It travels all over the fields. It moves through the forests, too. It also climbs up and over hills of dirt. A hedgehog is always searching for food. It feeds on soft worms. It also dines on crunchy insects! That is why it lives on the ground. A hole in the ground is a perfect home for a hedgehog!

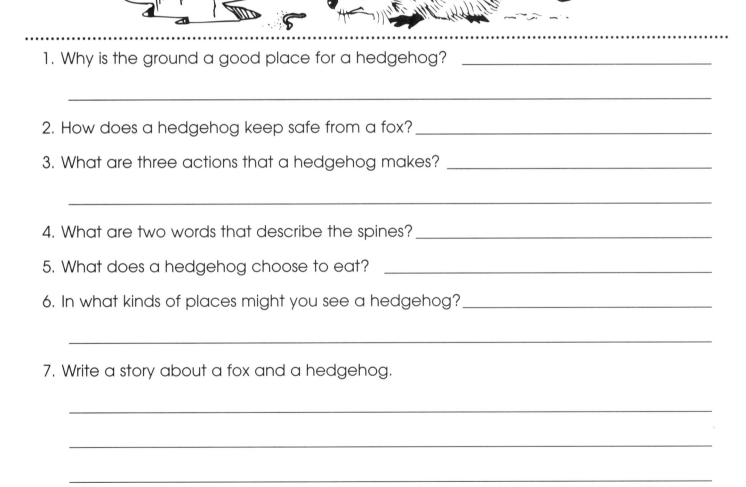

1. Why is the ground a good place for a hedgehog? _____

_____

2. How does a hedgehog keep safe from a fox? _____

3. What are three actions that a hedgehog makes? _____

_____

4. What are two words that describe the spines?_____

5. What does a hedgehog choose to eat? _____

6. In what kinds of places might you see a hedgehog?_____

_____

7. Write a story about a fox and a hedgehog.

_____

_____

_____

_____

_____

_____

Eel

There is a fish that looks more like a snake! It is called a moray eel. Read this poem about it.

A most ferocious kind of fish
Is called the moray eel.
It lurks around the coral reef
For the octopus—its meal!

Read these other facts about the moray eel.

A moray eel is very, very long and slippery.
A moray eel hatches from a small egg.
A moray eel can hurt people.

....

1. How is a moray eel different from other fish? _____

   _____

2. What kind of animal does a moray eel look like? _____

3. What does a moray eel eat? _____

   _____

4. What do you think *ferocious* means? _____

5. What word in the poem rhymes with *meal*? _____

6. Why wouldn't a diver want to see a moray eel? _____

   _____

7. Make a list of your own words to rhyme with *eel*.

   _____   _____

   _____   _____

   _____   _____

   _____   _____

   _____   _____

Flying Fish

Read this poem about a sea creature. This sea creature is a flying fish! Can a fish really fly?

When chased by hungry enemies,
It swishes with its tail,
Then spreads its fins to act like wings
And through the air will sail!

Yes, you see, there is a fish that can fly. It is a small fish, but it has huge fins. The fins look like the wings of a bird! The flying fish cannot flap like a bird, though. It just leaps up out of the sea. Then it can glide through the air. It can glide above the waves for about five feet.

....

1. What can a flying fish do? (three or four answers) _____

_____

_____

2. How is a flying fish like a bird? _____

_____

3. How is a flying fish different from a bird? _____

_____

4. When does this fish fly out of the water? _____

5. What does this fish do with its tail?_____

6. How does this fish fly?_____

_____

7. Imagine this flying fish being chased by a shark. Draw a picture.

The Octopus and the Worm

Each morning Grampa enjoyed walking beside the sea. He walked with a fishing pole in his hand. He walked out to the end of the pier. He said, "Good morning," to other fishermen. Then he put a worm on the hook. He dropped his fishing line into the sea. Then he waited. He waited to catch a fish on the hook.

"There's that worm again!" the octopus said beneath the sea. "Every morning I wake up and see a worm hanging down. It hangs down on a line. It dangles there by my cave!"

The octopus slid his slippery body away. He slid away from that worm! He did not know that the worm was for a fish. He just knew that a worm on a line meant trouble. The octopus felt danger from that dangling worm!

1. What do you think a "pier" is? _____

_____

2. What time of day did Grampa like to go to the pier? _____

3. Who did Grampa see each day? _____

_____

4. What two activities did Grampa enjoy? _____

_____

5. What is another word for *hangs*? _____

6. Why can an octopus slide very well? _____

_____

7. Why did the octopus slide away from the worm? _____

_____

Sea Turtles

A grown-up sea turtle is huge! It can weigh two hundred pounds! It is also strong. It has to be strong to swim in the ocean. A sea turtle is large and strong and heavy! The female sea turtle does not lay her eggs in the ocean. She swims to the shore to lay her eggs. She comes out of the ocean and digs a nest in the sand. She lays one hundred eggs in the nest in the sand! She covers her eggs with a lot of sand. The sand warms the eggs. The sand protects the eggs from birds. Some birds near the sea like to eat turtle eggs. When the eggs hatch, the new baby turtles try to get to the water. They crawl slowly in the sand. Birds fly down and eat the baby turtles! Only a few baby turtles get to the water safely. Then they begin their lives in the ocean.

1. What do some birds near the sea like to eat? _____

2. Why can the birds catch the baby turtles easily? _____

_____

3. Why does a sea turtle need to be strong? _____

4. Where does a sea turtle lay her eggs? _____

5. Why does she lay her eggs there? _____

6. Did you ever see a turtle? Write a story about a turtle.

_____

_____

_____

_____

_____

_____

_____

Jungle Safari

Safari Leader: Is this your first trip to Africa?

Young Boy: This is my second trip to Africa. My parents brought me here three years ago.

Safari Leader: Well, I'm happy to have you on my safari. Stay close to your parents now. We're ready to head out into the wild.

Young Boy: Wow! This is so cool! Is it okay if I use my camera?

Safari Leader: Sure. That's what we are here for! This is a photo shoot of lions in the bush.

Young Boy: Cool! Can you tell me how to spot the lions?

Safari Leader: Look for yellow or golden colors in the deep grass. Listen for a deep growl or roar. Watch for a flash of movement out in the open. Spot a water hole, and search for a lion there.

Young Boy: I know something about lions, too! I know they can be nine feet long!

1. What do you think *safari* means? _____

2. What is this group doing instead of hunting? _____

3. Do lions meow like a house cat? _____

4. What is a good place for lions to hide? _____

5. What is the length of a lion? _____

6. What are four ways to find a lion? _____

7. Would you like to go on a safari to Africa? Why or why not?

_____

_____

_____

_____

_____

Sea Horse

This is a poem about a fish. It is a fish that does not appear to be a fish. Its head looks like the head of a horse!

Not looking like a fish at all,
His tail ends in a curve.
He hooks his tail around a weed
So he can sway and swerve.

Here are some more facts about the sea horse:

A sea horse stands up to swim!
A sea horse has small fins on its head!
A sea horse lays 200 eggs at one time!

1. How do sea horses look different from other fish? _____

_____

2. How does the sea horse swim differently from other fish? _____

_____

3. What else is amazing about a sea horse? _____

_____

4. What kind of tail does a sea horse have? _____

_____

5. Why does a sea horse need a good tail? _____

_____

6. What do you think *sway* and *swerve* mean?_____

_____

7. In the poem, what word rhymes with *swerve*? _____

Opossum in the Moonlight

Clang! Bang! Clunk! The noises came from the backyard! The children woke up and called out. Father got out of bed, but he was still very sleepy. He and the children stepped quietly to the back door. The full moon gave light to the backyard. In the moonlight, the children saw an opossum eating garbage. The garbage was on the ground! The opossum had jumped up and tipped over the garbage can!

The opossum was one foot long. The tail was also one foot long. The opossum was hairy, but it had no hair on its tail! The nose was long and pointed. It was using its little hands to eat. It was eating old bits of fruit from the garbage can! The children watched the opossum for a few moments. Then Father put the children back into their cozy beds.

1. Why was there a noise in the night? _____

2. What was the total length of the opossum? _____

3. What do you think the word *moments* means? _____

   _____

4. Why could the children clearly see the opossum? _____

   _____

5. What is special about the opossum's tail? _____

   _____

6. Why did the opossum come to the backyard? _____

   _____

7. Did you ever hear or see an animal in the night? Tell about it.

   _____

   _____

   _____

   _____

Name _____

A Scuba Diver Sees a Squid

This is the story which Uncle Gary told me.

"I had gone to the ocean to do some scuba diving," said Uncle Gary. "I had my wet suit on and my flippers. My tank of oxygen was on my back, and I entered the sea. Down, down, down I dove. I dove down until it was very deep.

"I swam under the sea, and it was very beautiful," continued Uncle Gary. "Then I saw something strange. I saw a head and body with ten long arms! I counted the arms again," said Uncle Gary. "There were 10 arms, and they twisted around this way and that way. Then I watched the thing swim past me. I could see a beak on its face! I found out later that this strange creature was a squid," Uncle Gary finished.

1. What things did Uncle Gary need for scuba diving? _____

_____

2. How did Uncle Gary get down deep into the sea?_____

_____

3. What kind of creature did he see? _____

4. Why do you think he counted the creature's arms twice? _____

_____

5. How was the creature strange? _____

_____

6. What was Uncle Gary doing when he saw the squid? _____

_____

7. Imagine your own sea creature. Write about it.

_____

_____

_____

_____

_____

_____

Squirrel Grove

It was early one October morning. Dad finished flipping the pancakes. Anne and Joel finished eating the pancakes. They finished drinking their orange juice. Mother finished washing the pancake griddle.

"Let's drive to the mountains!" everybody said. "Let's visit Squirrel Grove!"

Their heavy, old truck followed the curves of the mountain road. Finally, they got close to the peak. That's where they could park the truck and walk through the squirrels' grove. Squirrels with full, swishing tails ran this way and that way. Gray, furry squirrels found acorns under the oak trees. Squirrels with busy, little paws played on the ground.

"There's a lot of hustle, bustle in Squirrel Grove," Anne said to Joel. "The squirrels are getting acorns before the winter comes!"

1. What do you think is another name for a cooking pan? _____

2. Who had the idea to go to the mountains? _____

3. What are three actions that the squirrels did? _____

   _____

4. What do you think the word *grove* means? _____

   _____

5. Where did the family park their truck? _____

6. What did you learn about squirrels in this story? _____

   _____

7. What do you think *hustle, bustle* means? _____

   _____

   _____

There Is a Dove

There is a bird called the dove. A dove is in the pigeon family. It is more beautiful than a pigeon, however. This beauty is because of its feathers. The dove's feathers have many different shades. There are shades of pink, purple, blue and gold on the feathers. The dove's body color is mostly light brown.

Most people are very surprised to see the dove's nest. The nest is not a soft, round thing. The nest of the dove is just a bunch of sticks and tiny twigs. The sticks and twigs are just lying on a flat surface above the ground. The dove is a beautiful bird, but its nest is not very pretty!

1. Find the word *shades* in the story. What does *shades* mean? _____

_____

2. What kind of bird is a dove? _____

3. Why is a dove so pretty? _____

4. What is surprising about a dove's nest? _____

_____

5. Where does a dove make a nest? _____

6. Can you think of other kinds of birds besides a dove or pigeon? _____

_____

7. Why are birds so interesting?

_____

_____

_____

_____

_____

Boogie Boarding

The August sun was bright! The morning was already hot! "We will go to the beach after breakfast," said Mom.

Dad packed the truck. Anita and Jose grabbed their colorful beach towels. "Who will get the first turn on the boogie board?" Dad asked. "We will flip a coin to see," laughed the children.

Jose won the coin toss! Time and again he pulled the boogie board out into the powerful surf and rode the waves to shore. He bounced and bumped on the strong waves! Salt water splashed on his face and hair. Finally, Anita could not wait any longer. She waded into the sea. The ocean pulled at her legs. She waved to Jose, and he steered the boogie board toward her. "It's my turn!" Anita shouted into the wind.

1. What did the children have to share? _____

2. Where do you go to use a boogie board? _____

3. What do you do on a boogie board? _____

_____

4. What did they take to the beach besides the boogie board? _____

_____

5. What are five actions words in this story? _____

_____

_____

6. How did they decide who got the boogie board first? _____

_____

7. What do you like to do in the summer? _____

_____

_____

_____

A Picnic Spot

It feels great to sit down and munch on a picnic lunch! You can enjoy a picnic in the park. You can enjoy a picnic at the beach. You can enjoy a picnic in your own yard. When you open your picnic basket, you know how fresh and good each bite will taste!

I have a place that is my favorite picnic spot. It is on the steps of a hard, high cliff above the sea. My family loves to share a picnic there! We each choose a different step to sit on. The sound of the crashing ocean waves is so loud that we cannot speak. We just listen to the power of the sea. We taste the salt of the sea with each bite of our lunch. We can relax and think and dream on the steps of the cliff above the sea!

1. What are three nice places to have a picnic? _____

_____

2. Describe the cliff in this story. _____

3. What is interesting about being at the ocean? _____

_____

4. Why doesn't this family speak during their picnic? _____

_____

5. How does their picnic lunch taste different in that place? _____

6. Why does this family like to have a picnic on the cliff above the sea? _____

_____

7. Plan a picnic lunch. Write down everything you want to have in your own picnic basket.

_____   _____

_____   _____

_____   _____

_____   _____

A Table Game

Ping-Pong™ is a fun game to play! People use a special table to play Ping-Pong™. There is a tiny net across the middle of the table. That is why some people call this game "table tennis." A real tennis game, however, has a net on the ground across a large court. In a real tennis game, people hit a fuzzy rubber ball with a racquet. In a table tennis game, people hit a smooth plastic ball with a paddle.

To play "table tennis" or Ping-Pong™, each person needs a paddle. The game also requires a very small ball. This ball is not very heavy. It is light, and it can bounce high and fast. Each person tries to hit the ball across the net. It is important for the ball to stay on the table! There are lines on the Ping-Pong™ table. The ball also needs to stay inside the lines. Control of your power is important in this exciting game.

1. What is another name for Ping-Pong™? _____

2. What are some ways Ping-Pong™ is different from real tennis? _____

_____

3. Why can a Ping-Pong™ ball bounce high and fast? _____

_____

4. Why does a Ping-Pong™ table have lines? _____

_____

5. Name five other sports you can play with a ball.

_____

_____

_____

_____

_____

18

Ice Skating

In the past, people in the cold, cold North used ice skates. They used ice skates for traveling! They used ice skates to get from one place to another. People would skate across a frozen river. They would skate across to visit a friend on the other side! In the past, ice skates were made from animal bones. People just strapped animal bones to their footwear. Then they could glide across the ice!

Today, most people use ice skates for sports. To ice skate on a frozen pond is exciting! To race on ice skates is a thrill! To play hockey on ice skates is wonderful! Today, ice skates are made in a factory. Workers in a factory put blades of steel on the bottom of special boots. With these skates, a person can step and slide and glide on the ice.

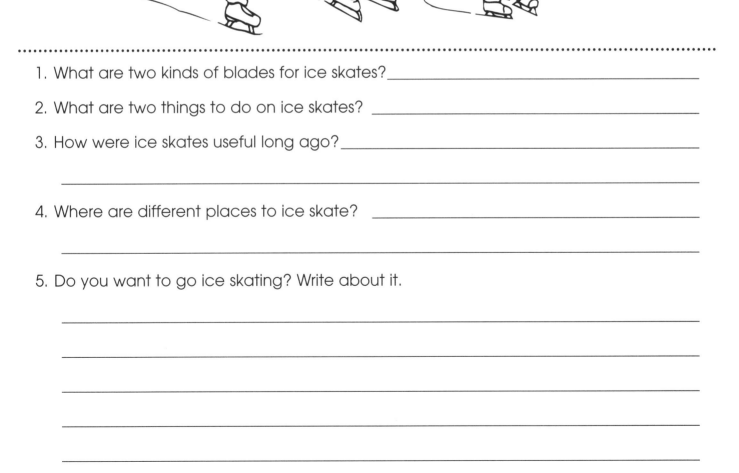

1. What are two kinds of blades for ice skates? _____

2. What are two things to do on ice skates? _____

3. How were ice skates useful long ago? _____

_____

4. Where are different places to ice skate? _____

_____

5. Do you want to go ice skating? Write about it.

_____

_____

_____

_____

_____

Badminton

Set up the net;
Call the new friend you met!

One on each side;
The yard is quite wide!

A racquet in hand;
This game is grand!

Give the birdie a toss;
Now a win or a loss!

Whiz! Whack! Whir!
A game for him or her!

1. What three things do you need for badminton? _____

_____

2. Who can play this game? _____

3. Where can you play badminton? _____

4. How do you get ready for this game? _____

_____

5. What word rhymes with *wide*? _____

6. What is a sound that this game makes? _____

7. Tell about a game that you like to play.

_____

_____

_____

_____

_____

Fishing from the Dock

They saw the boat dock by the shore of the lake. Three shiny motorboats were tied to the boat dock. One old, wooden rowboat was also tied to the dock.

They walked out to the end of the boat dock. They looked down into the deep, cool water. The water was active with many fish swimming this way and that way!

"This is a super place to try our luck!" Shamus said to Eddie.

They set down their poles and their buckets of minnows. Then they did what Dad had said. They put on their life jackets and tied the straps! Now they could fish from the dock.

The two fish that Eddie caught were big ones. They were big enough to take home and fry. The three fish that Shamus caught were big enough to win a prize!

1. How were the fish in the lake swimming? _____

2. In what way is a boat dock useful? _____

_____

3. What does it mean *to try our luck*? _____

_____

4. What three things did the boys have with them?_____

_____

5. Why did the boys put life jackets on? _____

_____

6. Can you write a story about catching a fish?

_____

_____

_____

_____

_____

Just Floating

In the heat of the summer, most children like to splash and swim. Did you ever try just floating? Floating is wonderful! It is especially nice to float on your back! If you float on your back, you can relax your body. You can also relax your mind. Just float and dream as the clouds go by.

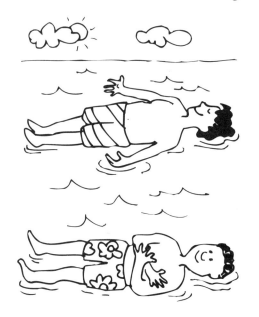

On a blazing, hot day
I head for the pool.

Leaping into the water
I shout, "It feels cool."

I float on my back
With a smile on my face,

Looking up at the sky—
It's a beautiful place!

I rest as I float;
My heart feels joy—

Floating is fine
For girl or boy.

1. Why is floating good for you? _____

2. In the story part, what are four actions? _____

    _____

3. In the poem, what word rhymes with *place*? _____

4. What line rhymes with *my heart feels joy*? _____

    _____

5. What can you do as you float? _____

6. On this page, what are two other words for *hot*? _____

7. What do you know about floating?

    _____

    _____

    _____

The Game of Football

The game of football is exciting to watch and very, very physical to play. Eleven players form each team, and two teams oppose each other. The two teams play on a field that is 100 yards long. That is a distance of 300 feet! That is quite a distance to run back and forth! There are zones at each end of the field. These areas are called end zones! The end zones are where touchdowns take place.

The football game begins with a kickoff by one team. The other team receives the kickoff and runs with the ball. The team makes a touchdown if it can move the football all the way to the end zone. The crowd cheers loudly for the team that makes a touchdown. The touchdown is worth six points. Then the team can try for one extra point by kicking the football over the goal.

1. What is special about the end zones? _____

2. What do you think the word *oppose* means? _____

   _____

3. Why is a touchdown exciting? _____

4. Why is a football game very, very physical? _____

   _____

   _____

5. What is the length of a football field? _____

6. How does the crowd take part in the game? _____

7. Do you like to play any kinds of ball? Write about why you do or do not like to play ball.

   _____

   _____

   _____

   _____

Our P.E. Class

"Hello, boys and girls. I am Miss Ling. I am your P.E. teacher this year. I want to tell you about my P.E. program. I also need to explain some rules about P.E. class. First of all, you will come to P.E. three times a week. It will be a chance to have fun. It will also be a time to learn some new rules.

"When you come to class, put on your sneakers. Boots or sandals will not be allowed. If you have long hair, please tie it back. I don't allow any food, snacks or chewing gum. Water is important, though. The drinking fountains are right over there.

"I will teach you many sports and activities. Some of them will be Ping-Pong™, four square, softball, soccer and tumbling. You will notice your balance improve. You will also gain strength. This class will be physical! That's what *Physical Education* means!

1. What did Miss Ling talk about? _____

_____

2. What are some of Miss Ling's rules? _____

_____

3. How will Miss Ling's P.E. class help you? _____

_____

4. What do you think *gain strength* means? _____

_____

5. What are five things that Miss Ling does not allow?_____

_____

_____

6. Think of two more rules for P.E. (your own ideas). _____

_____

7. Make a list of six other physical activities (not from this story).

_____   _____

_____   _____

_____   _____

Hiking

To hike is to take a long walk outdoors. There are many wonderful places to take a hike. You can hike around a lake. You can hike up and down hills. You can hike on a trail through the woods. You can hike across a field or meadow. You can hike along the path of a stream.

Here are some rules to remember if you go hiking:

Do not ever hike alone. Hike with your family.
Take a whistle with you when you hike.
Carry a water bottle or canteen when you hike.
Have a first-aid kit with you when you hike.
Plan your hike, and then tell a friend where your family will hike.

1. Find four groups of words that tell where to hike. _____

_____

_____

2. What can you take instead of a water bottle? _____

3. What does *hiking* mean? _____

_____

4. What do you think is in the first-aid kit? _____

_____

5. What do you need to do before you go hiking? _____

_____

6. Why must you never hike alone? Write about it.

_____

_____

_____

_____

_____

_____

Grass

Little Brown Ant:	Winter is gone! The snow is gone!
Ladybug:	The grass is beginning to sprout!
Little Brown Ant:	There is grass here! There is grass there!
Ladybug:	This will be a front yard again!
Little Brown Ant:	The grass smells good! The grass smells fresh!
Ladybug:	The whole world looks new in the spring!
Little Brown Ant:	I feel a sprinkle of rain! The rain will make the grass grow tall!
Ladybug::	The grass feels cool! The grass feels soft!
Little Brown Ant:	Let's dash through the grass!
Ladybug:	You run fast, and I will follow you! I will chase you through the new grass!
Little Brown Ant:	The grass is so green! The grass is so clean!
Ladybug:	I will hide, and you can seek me in the grass!

1. What is so nice about the grass in the spring? _____

_____

2. What two sentences rhyme with each other? _____

_____

3. What two games do they play in the grass? _____

_____

4. What do you think *sprout* means? _____

_____

5. What is the change of seasons in this story? _____

6. What is another word for *run* in this story? _____

7. Write about how you have fun in the grass.

_____

_____

_____

_____

The Pond

"Hello, boys and girls. I'm so happy that you came here with your teacher! This is Green Grass Park, and I am the park ranger here. Today I want to show you the pond. It is right over there. Let's walk over to the pond together.

"Look! Isn't it a wonderful pond? It is alive with life! Stand very still, and watch carefully. You will see what I mean. There! Did you see the pretty, blue wings of the dragonfly? Now look at the edge of the water. A tiny snake is sliding in to have a sip of pond water. Watch the grass moving, too! A turtle is in the grass. It is taking slow, sure steps from the pond. This pond is a beautiful part of our planet Earth!"

1. Who took the children to Green Grass Park? _____

2. How do you know where the turtle is? _____

_____

3. Who hikes with the children to the pond? _____

4. Name three things near the pond that are alive. _____

_____

5. Why does the snake want to go to the pond? _____

_____

6. Why is a pond an important place on our planet Earth?

_____

_____

_____

_____

_____

Flowers in the Wild

Many flowers grow in the wild. They do not need to be planted. Nobody needs to water them. They do not want a garden or even a pot. They just want to grow. They are called wildflowers, and they are lovely! Wildflowers grow in open fields. They grow in grassy meadows. They grow on the sides of hills and mountains. They just grow! Mother Nature gives them the care that they need!

It is not a good idea to pick a bunch of wildflowers. Wildflowers continue to grow by dropping their own seeds. That is why people should not pick them. Healthy wild-flowers are ones that are left alone!

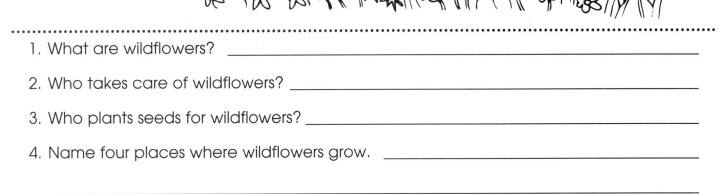

1. What are wildflowers? _____

2. Who takes care of wildflowers? _____

3. Who plants seeds for wildflowers? _____

4. Name four places where wildflowers grow. _____

_____

5. Draw a picture of wildflowers growing.

Low Tide

Two children went with Aunt Susan to the beach. Aunt Susan knew the best time to go the beach. "We will arrive at the beach at low tide," Aunt Susan told the children as they rode in her red van. "Low tide at the beach is so much fun," Aunt Susan said, and she smiled.

Aunt Susan stopped her red van on Beach Avenue. Carefully, the three of them crossed the road. Then they all ran as fast as rabbits to the sand! "It is low tide," Aunt Susan shouted in the wind. "See how the ocean has pulled back from the shore? That is why you will find so many shells and rocks on the beach! The ocean gives you a chance at low tide," said Aunt Susan. "It is a chance to find treasures from the sea!"

1. What is the best time to pick up shells and rocks at the beach? _____

2. How did the children get to the beach? _____

3. What is special about low tide? _____

   _____

4. What are some treasures from the sea? _____

   _____

5. What did they have to be careful about? _____

   _____

6. What did they do to show their excitement? _____

7. Write what you know about finding shells and rocks.

   _____

   _____

   _____

   _____

   _____

Desert

A desert does not get much rain. Grass does not grow well in a desert. Few plants grow in the desert. These plants are able to hold the little amount of rain that they get. That small amount of rain will help these plants survive. The animals of the desert also do not need much water to stay alive. Some animals eat the desert plants.

Most of the desert is just sand. There are also some rocks in the desert. There are broken rocks called stones, too. Some of the stones are broken into smaller pieces called gravel. Now you know why it is hard, dry and rough to take a walk in the desert.

1. Why is it difficult for anything to live in a desert? _____

_____

2. What do rocks break down to form? _____

3. How are plants able to survive in the desert? _____

_____

4. Why is a desert so hard, dry and rough? _____

5. How do animals of the desert get enough water? _____

_____

6. What does gravel come from? _____

7. Write something else that you know about a desert.

_____

_____

_____

_____

_____

Forest

There was a sign that said: Pine Forest. That is where Dad stopped the car. We got out of the car and saw a dirt path that led into the forest. It was fun to walk on that path. It was not a straight path. It went around this way and around that way. I felt excited! This was my first time in any forest, and it was a big adventure to me! I found a pinecone under a tall tree. Then I found an old, dry skin of a long, thin snake. The forest was beautiful and very quiet. It felt peaceful there. Now I know something new. I know why animals of the forest love their forest home!

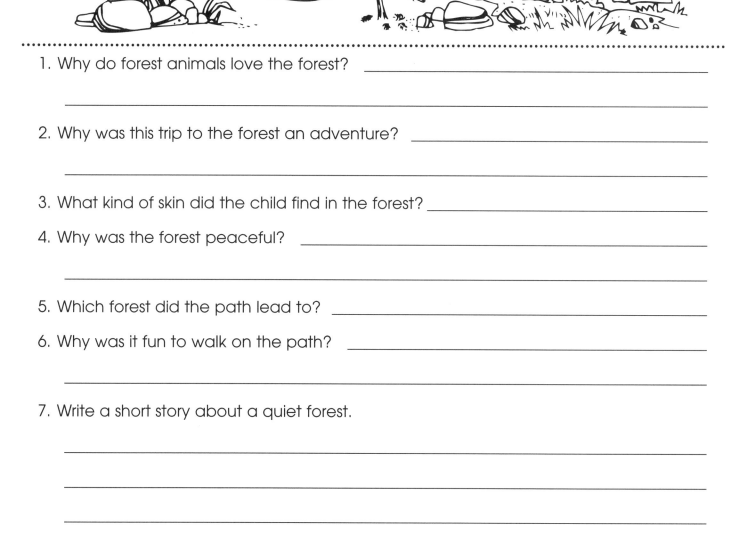

1. Why do forest animals love the forest? _____

_____

2. Why was this trip to the forest an adventure? _____

_____

3. What kind of skin did the child find in the forest? _____

4. Why was the forest peaceful? _____

_____

5. Which forest did the path lead to? _____

6. Why was it fun to walk on the path? _____

_____

7. Write a short story about a quiet forest.

_____

_____

_____

_____

_____

Trees

I think the most beautiful living things are trees. Trees are the best things on our
planet Earth to me!

Trees with lemons give us cool juice to drink.
Trees with leaves are so pretty, I think.
Trees with nuts give us something fun to crack.
Trees with apples give us a tasty snack.
Trees with oranges give us fruit to eat.
Trees with plums give us something sweet.

Trees are nice to sit under. They provide shade on a hot, sunny day. Trees are tall and
strong. They are alive and growing all of the time. Some trees live and grow for two
thousand years!

1. Name three fruits that trees give us. _____

_____

2. Why is a tree nice on a very hot day? _____

_____

3. What do trees give that is not a fruit? _____

4. What is a very old age for a tree? _____

5. In the poem, what word rhymes with *snack*? _____

6. Write down what you like about trees.

_____

_____

_____

_____

_____

_____

A Town in the Valley

From the big highway, you can see a narrow road. That road leads into the valley. From the big highway, you can see it all. You can see how strong hills surround the valley. You can feel that the hills protect the valley.

There are homes in the valley. Many stores and schools make this place a town! In the center of this town is a church. This church is more than one hundred years old! Cowboys and their families built this church long ago. Back then, hundreds of families came to live in this town in the valley. Now there are thousands of families who live there. Each day they feel the strength from the hills around them. The strong hills surround this valley town!

1. When did cowboys come to live in this town? _____

2. What makes this place a town? _____

   _____

3. What is another word for *strong* in this story? _____

4. Why are the hills important in this story? _____

   _____

5. How do you know this town had grown larger? _____

   _____

6. How do you know there are hills on more than one side of this town? _____

   _____

7. On a piece of paper draw a picture of this story. Add anything extra to the picture that you would like.

What Is a Brook?

This brook is the beginning of a river. This brook is not wide and fast flowing. It is narrow and very, very gentle. A small child with a parent could play near this brook. This brook is not powerful. It gives you a peaceful feeling.

You can follow the path of this brook for many, many miles. You might find the place where the brook begins to widen. This is where the brook changes to a stream. The stream flows a little faster than the brook. The stream is wider than the brook, too. You can follow the path of the stream. After many, many miles the stream changes to a very wide, fast-flowing river. The river began as a gentle brook.

1. What is nice about a brook? _____

2. What two things are wider than a brook? _____

3. What is bigger than a brook but smaller than a river? _____

4. How do some rivers begin? _____

5. What do you think *widen* means? _____

6. Why is a brook a peaceful place? _____

7. Draw a picture of a brook, a stream and a river.

Mountains

A mountain is larger than a hill. The top of a mountain is called a peak. Some mountain peaks are famous. Famous mountain peaks have names! Two famous peaks are Pikes Peak and Mount Everest. Pikes Peak is in the United States. Everest is a mountain peak in a country called Nepal. Nepal is near India.

Mountains are interesting because of their age. Many mountains are millions of years old. Mountains are also interesting because of their height. The height of a mountain tells how high it is. Some mountains are more than 25,000 feet high! These high mountains are sometimes covered by clouds in the sky!

1. What famous peak is near India? _____

2. What mountain peak is in North America? _____

3. Why do clouds cover some mountains? _____

   _____

4. What is the height of a very high mountain? _____

5. Why is a hill not called a mountain? _____

   _____

6. Some mountains are covered with grass or trees. Some mountains are covered with rocks. Some mountains are covered with ice. Some mountains are covered with snow. What kinds of mountains do you like best? Why?

   _____

   _____

   _____

   _____

   _____

   _____

Nature's Material

There is so much material in nature! Many people use nature's material for their own collections. People make collections of leaves from nature. People make collections of rocks from nature. Some people make collections of pinecones.

Besides making good collections, nature's material is wonderful for art! Flower petals are pretty to put in a dish or tray. Nuts can be used to fill a bowl or a basket. Some people use weeds to decorate a house! Weeds are nice for setting in a vase or empty jug. Other people prefer picking berries. They dry the berries to make an art display. Art displays from natural materials are very pretty.

1. Name five natural materials in this story. _____

_____

2. What are weeds good for? _____

_____

3. What are dried berries used for? _____

_____

4. What are six containers named in this story? _____

_____

5. Can you think of more containers? _____

_____

6. Do you collect anything from nature? _____

7. Where is a good place to look for natural materials?

_____

_____

Gold in Alaska

More than one hundred years ago, Roy Dane lived in Alaska. Roy Dane was a cowboy without a family. He knew that there was gold deep in the Earth. He lived his whole life digging for that gold. How he worked! How he searched!

Roy Dane was not afraid of cold and dark places. He dug tunnels deep into the ground. In the dark of the tunnels, he worked. His clothes and boots were covered with dirt. He shook the dirt off and worked some more. Did Roy Dane find gold in Alaska? Yes, he found some gold, and then his luck ran out.

1. What was Roy Dane searching for? _____

2. Where was he searching? _____

3. What was it like in the tunnels? _____

_____

4. Why do you think gold is a good treasure? _____

_____

5. Why is it not easy to find gold? _____

_____

6. What does *his luck ran out* mean? _____

_____

7. What do you think he did when his luck ran out?

_____

_____

_____

_____

_____

A Writer and Artist

Did you ever hear of a writer named Roger DuVoisin? He wrote some great story-books! Two of his books are *The Happy Lion* and *Donkey-Donkey*. He drew the pictures for those books, too! *Donkey-Donkey* is a funny book about a donkey on a farm. That donkey was not happy. He was not happy because he did not like his ears. He wanted to have ears on the side of his head. He did not like his ears on the top of his head!

Many years ago Roger DuVoisin wanted to study art for his work. He went to art school. He learned how to paint posters, and he made designs, too. Later, he learned to make pottery. After that, he learned how to make drawings for storybooks. You will enjoy his drawings and his stories! Look for books by Roger DuVoisin in your library.

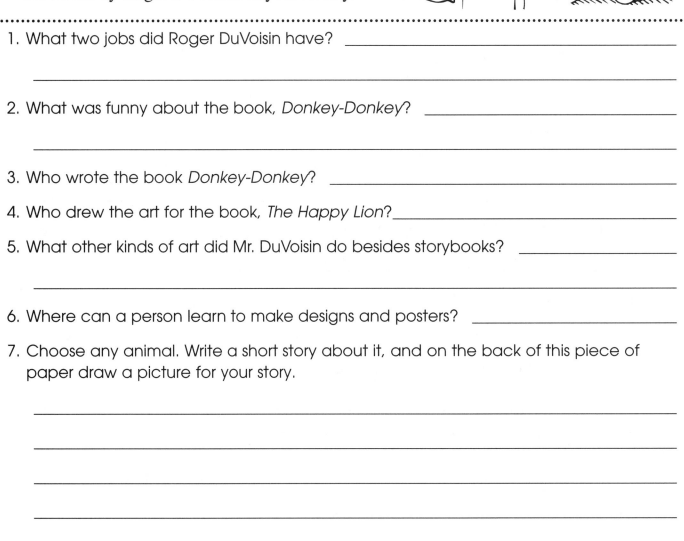

1. What two jobs did Roger DuVoisin have? _____

_____

2. What was funny about the book, *Donkey-Donkey*? _____

_____

3. Who wrote the book *Donkey-Donkey*? _____

4. Who drew the art for the book, *The Happy Lion*? _____

5. What other kinds of art did Mr. DuVoisin do besides storybooks? _____

_____

6. Where can a person learn to make designs and posters? _____

7. Choose any animal. Write a short story about it, and on the back of this piece of paper draw a picture for your story.

_____

_____

_____

_____

_____

My Work as a Firefighter

"Good afternoon, boys and girls! I'm so happy that you could come to the fire station on your field trip. My name is Chris, and I am going to discuss my work as a fire-fighter. I will also let you climb up on the pumper truck, but only three children at a time. The pumper truck has a lot of heavy hoses on it. Please be careful, and watch your step.

"There! Did each one of you have a turn up on the pumper truck? My job is to drive that truck to the scene of a fire. Sometimes, we arrive at accident scenes, also. The work of my team is to save people's lives. We work to save people's property. We are brave, and we are very strong. We must be strong to pull and support those heavy hoses. When those hoses are filled with water, they are powerful. The force of the water can put a fire out."

1. What does the word *discuss* mean? _____

_____

2. What does the word *scene* mean? _____

_____

3. What is a fire truck with hoses called? _____

4. Where do pumper trucks go? (two answers) _____

_____

5. Why must firefighters be strong? _____

_____

6. What were the children allowed to do? _____

7. Make a list of things a firefighter can save. (List six or seven ideas.)

_____   _____

_____   _____

_____   _____

_____

Sacagawea

More than two hundred years ago a woman named Sacagawea lived in America. She was a young and strong Native American. She knew the land and the rivers and the mountains very well. She also knew the plants and the animals. She was very brave.

Sacagawea helped a group of men. She helped the men to explore America. She helped the men explore from South Dakota to the Pacific Ocean. They all went west together.

Sacagawea showed the men how to find berries and roots to eat. She showed them how to make good use of animal skins. She showed them a way to live during the icy, cold winters. She helped them make friends with the Native Americans. The men were able to survive and to learn about the West with help from Sacagawea.

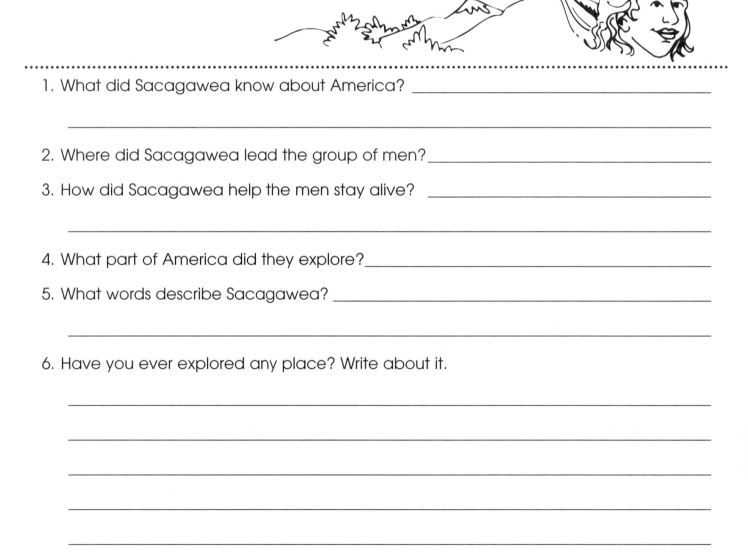

1. What did Sacagawea know about America? _____

_____

2. Where did Sacagawea lead the group of men? _____

3. How did Sacagawea help the men stay alive? _____

_____

4. What part of America did they explore? _____

5. What words describe Sacagawea? _____

_____

6. Have you ever explored any place? Write about it.

_____

_____

_____

_____

_____

Two Smart Professors

Next door to my house is a very busy family. The mother and father are both college professors. They have one little girl, and she dreams of becoming a professor, too! Sometimes people ask me who my neighbors are. I always say, "My neighbors are two smart professors!"

Those two smart professors spend a lot of time reading. I know that because I have seen their books. They put stacks of books on the floor! They cover shelves on the wall with books! They set books on the tables and books on the windowsills! They read, and they learn. They read, and they understand. They have to know a lot. They teach at a college. They are two smart professors!

1. Why do you think the professors are so smart? _____

_____

2. Where are four places they keep their books? _____

_____

3. Who has a dream to become a professor? _____

4. What happens when you read a lot? _____

_____

5. Besides reading a lot, what do the professors do? _____

_____

6. What are four action verbs in this story? _____

_____

7. When you read, what do you want to learn about?

_____

_____

_____

_____

Helicopter Pilot

Many girls and boys dream about becoming pilots. Here is a super dream. Become a helicopter pilot! A helicopter pilot must be smart. A helicopter pilot must be brave. A helicopter pilot must be able to be trusted. It is not easy to be a helicopter pilot. The job is a special one!

A helicopter pilot has to train for the job. The training takes long, hard weeks and months. A helicopter is a complex machine to handle. However, a helicopter can do important work. A pilot can fly a helicopter from the deck of a ship. A pilot can fly a helicopter to a hospital emergency room. A pilot can fly a helicopter over a forest fire. A helicopter pilot is a person to respect!

1. Who can become a helicopter pilot? _____

2. Why is it difficult to become a helicopter pilot? _____

_____

3. Write two words to describe a helicopter pilot. _____

4. What do you think *complex* means? _____

_____

5. Why does a helicopter pilot need to be brave? _____

_____

6. Why do people respect helicopter pilots? _____

_____

7. Write a short story about a helicopter pilot.

_____

_____

_____

_____

_____

Mrs. John Adams

More than two hundred years ago, George Washington was the President. He was the first President of the United States of America. Do you know who the second President of the U.S.A. was? The second President was a man named John Adams. His wife was Abigail Adams. Mrs. Abigail Adams was a very important woman!

Mrs. Adams was important for many reasons. She was important because she was the President's wife. She was important because she raised three children. She was important because she was the one to pay the bills and take care of the farm when her husband was away. She was also important because she wrote more than 2000 letters in her lifetime! Those letters are still on file in Washington, D.C. Something else important happened. Mrs. Adams did not know about this, though. After she died, her son became the sixth President of the U.S.A.!

1. Who was John Adams?_____

2. Who was Mrs. Abigail Adams? _____

3. Who was the sixth President of the United States? _____

4. What was one important duty of Mrs. Abigail Adams? _____

_____

5. How do you know that her letters were important, too? _____

_____

6. How many important jobs did Mrs. Abigail Adams have?_____

_____

7. What do you think a President's wife has to do today?

_____

_____

_____

_____

A Smart Queen

Long, long ago a woman lived who had the name Cleopatra. Cleopatra was a pretty woman who was also very smart. She was the Queen of Egypt more than 2000 years ago! As the Queen, she had everything that she wanted. She had fancy clothing and jewels, and she had many friends. Two of her friends were Roman leaders. Rome was a country near Egypt.

Cleopatra was also called the Queen of the Nile. The Nile was a long river that flowed through Egypt. (The Nile River still flows through Egypt today.) Cleopatra's palace was near the Nile River. She lived there with many people to serve her and to entertain her. In her court she had people to play music for her. She also had people to cook for her and even to dress her!

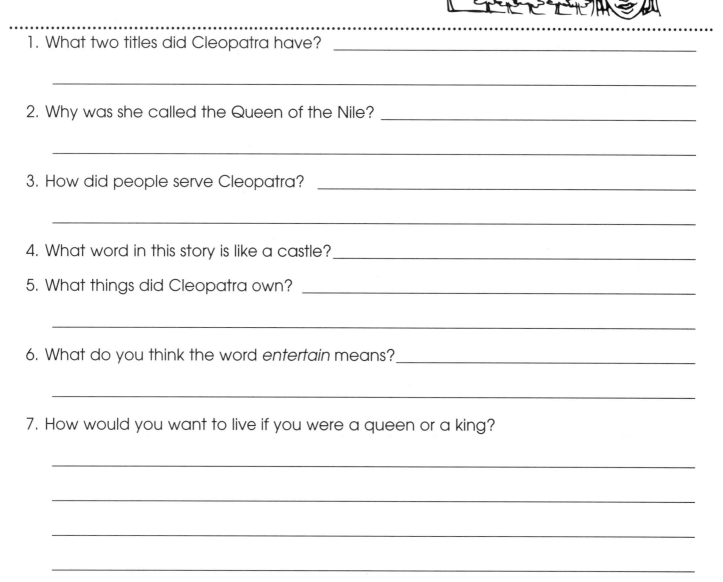

1. What two titles did Cleopatra have? _____

_____

2. Why was she called the Queen of the Nile? _____

_____

3. How did people serve Cleopatra? _____

_____

4. What word in this story is like a castle? _____

5. What things did Cleopatra own? _____

_____

6. What do you think the word *entertain* means? _____

_____

7. How would you want to live if you were a queen or a king?

_____

_____

_____

_____

44

The Market Man

In the busy, busy city there is a market on the corner. It is a fresh fish market. The market man owns the market. He has important work to do. Very early each morning the market man goes to the ocean. He meets fishermen there. He buys only the best fish for his market. He chooses the best fish for you and for me.

The market man's brother has a fresh market out in the country. It is a fruit market. He also sells vegetables there. Sometimes he has fresh honey from the bee farm at his market. His work is important. Every morning he visits the nearby farms. He talks with the farmers. He selects perfect fruit from the farmers. He takes the nicest vegetables. He puts them in his market to sell to you and to me.

1. What is the same about the two brothers' jobs? _____

_____

2. What is different about their jobs? _____

_____

3. Why are the mornings very important for both brothers? _____

_____

4. Where is the market in the city located? _____

_____

5. What do you think the word *select* means? _____

_____

6. What kind of fish does the market man in the city sell? _____

7. Make a list of three foods to buy at the country market.

_____

Jill Tang, M.D.

I always admire my Aunt Jill. She is a medical doctor. That is why her office door shows her name this way: Jill Tang, M.D. *M.D.* means "medical doctor." Sometimes I see her sign her name another way: Dr. Jill Tang. *Dr.* is a short way to write *doctor*.

I go to see Dr. Jill Tang whenever I am sick. She is my aunt, and I am her nephew. However, she treats me just like any other patient. She listens to my heart pumping blood. She asks me to breathe deeply. Then she listens to the air go through my lungs. She makes me stick out my tongue. Then she takes a look at my throat. She even tells me to look at the eye chart. That way she can check my vision. I like to go to Dr. Tang's office! I always feel better after she examines me!

1. Who is telling the story? _____

2. How do you know that Jill Tang is a medical doctor? _____

   _____

3. Name four parts of the body Dr. Tang checks. _____

   _____

4. What part of the body is used for breathing? _____

5. What do you think *vision* means? _____

   _____

6. How does Dr. Tang check the throat? _____

   _____

7. Write about your experience visiting a doctor.

   _____

   _____

   _____

   _____

The Tailor's Hands

Uncle Jack is a tailor, and I have watched him work. Uncle Jack has strong and busy hands. His hands must be strong because he cuts and sews all day long. He cuts and sews cloth to make clothing. He snips and he clips at the cloth. When he gets it just right, he begins to piece it together. He stitches and sews, and he sews and he stitches. Finally, the new clothing is ready! The tailor has made it!

Part of Uncle Jack's work is to take orders. People call Uncle Jack to order new clothing. He makes the clothing fit each person exactly right. He sews custom clothing to fit each person. He creates clothing for tall people, tiny people, heavy people, slim people—people of every size and shape! A tailor's work is a form of art, and Uncle Jack loves his work!

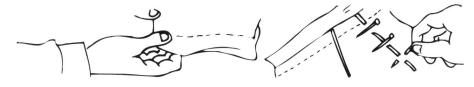

1. What do you think *snip and clip* means? _____

_____

2. What is the difference between cloth and clothing? _____

_____

3. How is the work of a tailor a form of art? _____

_____

4. Which word describes thin people? _____

5. Why are Uncle Jack's hands so busy? _____

_____

6. What are five action verbs in this story? _____

_____

7. List supplies you think a tailor would use.

_____   _____

_____   _____

_____   _____

Learning Can Be a Hobby

Hector is a boy who likes to learn. He likes to learn many things. For Hector, learning is his hobby! He spends a lot of time on this hobby. Imagine how much he learns!

Hector learns how things work. He can take a toy apart and put it back together. That way, he finds out how that toy works. He learns how things react. He can start one action and wait for the reaction. Reactions are part of science. So, it is Hector's hobby to learn about science. Sometimes, he wants to learn more about math. He adds up numbers, and subtracts them—just for fun! His hobby is always to learn something new! Nothing is boring to him. Everything that he learns is exciting!

1. Why does this boy learn so much? _____

_____

2. What can he learn from a toy? _____

_____

3. What can he learn about an action? _____

_____

4. How does he make math fun? _____

_____

5. In this story, what word is the opposite of *boring*? _____

6. What is this boy's hobby? _____

7. What do you like to learn? Do you spend a lot of time on it? Is that your hobby?

_____

_____

_____

_____

_____

_____

Seeds to Order

When you eat fruit you find seeds, of course! You find seeds in the core of an apple. You find seeds in the fruit of an orange. You even find teeny, tiny seeds in a banana. Did you ever think about ordering seeds? Some people look through magazines to find seeds to order! My grampa does.

My grampa lives in a very cold place. He likes to dream during the winter. He dreams about planting seeds when spring comes. The weather warms up in the spring, and it is a great time for planting. My grampa's hobby is choosing seeds to order. He orders them from a company. Then the company sends the seeds to him. The seeds arrive at Grampa's apartment in little packages. Grampa waits with excitement for spring. Then he begins planting his seeds!

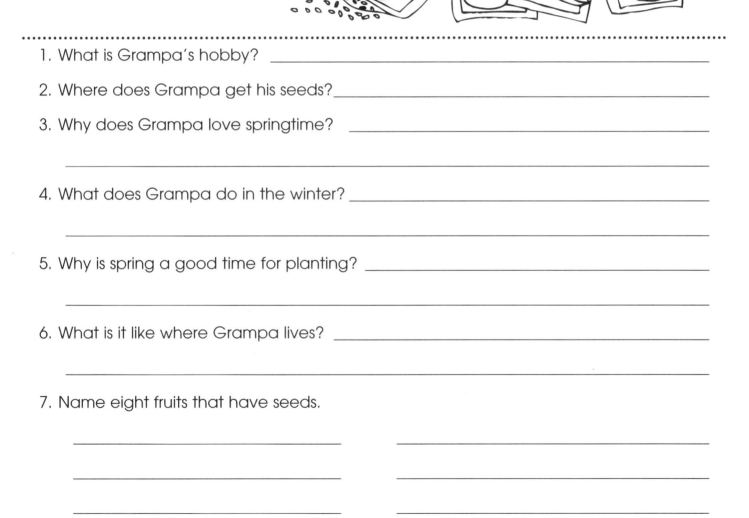

1. What is Grampa's hobby? _____

2. Where does Grampa get his seeds? _____

3. Why does Grampa love springtime? _____

   _____

4. What does Grampa do in the winter? _____

   _____

5. Why is spring a good time for planting? _____

   _____

6. What is it like where Grampa lives? _____

   _____

7. Name eight fruits that have seeds.

   _____   _____

   _____   _____

   _____   _____

   _____   _____

Rocks and Shells

It is an exciting hobby to collect rocks and shells. To gather rocks and shells is to take a part of the Earth. There are a variety of places to find rocks and shells. Rocks and shells are by the river. Rocks and shells are at the sea. Rocks and shells are on the shore of the bay.

There are many projects to do with rocks and shells. Put some rocks and shells in your garden. Place some rocks and shells on a pretty plate. Arrange some rocks and shells on your windowsill. Lay some rocks and shells under a tree. Most of all, enjoy the rocks and shells that you find!

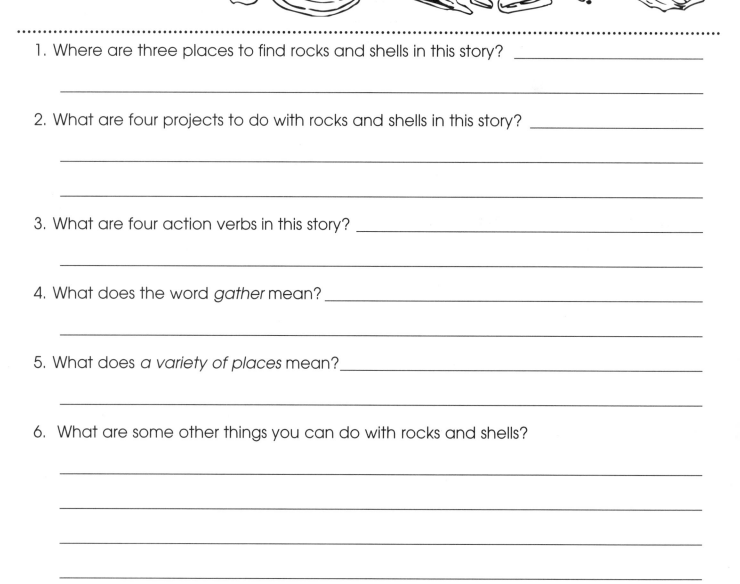

1. Where are three places to find rocks and shells in this story? _____

_____

2. What are four projects to do with rocks and shells in this story? _____

_____

_____

3. What are four action verbs in this story? _____

_____

4. What does the word *gather* mean? _____

_____

5. What does *a variety of places* mean?_____

_____

6. What are some other things you can do with rocks and shells?

_____

_____

_____

Reading as a Hobby

Reading! It is a cool hobby. People of all ages choose reading as a hobby. Many people choose storybooks to read. Stories are called fiction. Other people choose history or news to read. This is called non-fiction.

There is a great story to read called "Who's There." A lady named Miriam Potter wrote this story. The main character in this story is Mrs. Goose. This story is about a noise in her closet. Mrs. Goose is frightened by the noise in her closet. Mrs. Goose asks her friends to help her. She asks them to poke around in her closet. By poking around, they discover what is making the scary sound. This story will make you laugh!

1. What two kinds of books do people read? _____

2. What are some kinds of non-fiction? _____

_____

3. What did Miriam Potter write?_____

_____

4. Where does the story "Who's There" take place? _____

5. What is the mystery in the story "Who's There"? _____

_____

6. Is the story about Mrs. Goose a scary story? How do you know? _____

_____

7. Write about a story or a book that you like.

_____

_____

_____

_____

Mother's Pies

For some mothers, cooking is hard work. Maybe baking is hard work, too. Not for our mother! Our mother enjoys cooking and baking. Those are her hobbies! Her favorite hobby is baking pies. Her hobby is baking pies, and our hobby is eating them. We just love our mother's pies!

Mother has many recipes for making pies. Three of those recipes are our favorites. First, we love mother's apple pie. Mother chops up 14 fresh apples to make her apple pie! Second, we love mother's banana cream pie. She uses vanilla pudding and two good bananas to make that pie. It is smooth and sweet! Our third favorite pie is mother's lemon pie. That is a wonderful pie! It is quite tart, though! She uses one juicy lemon and a cup of sour cream to make her lemon pie. Mother has a good hobby! Her hobby is making pies.

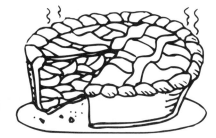

1. Why do the children enjoy their mother's hobby? _____

_____

2. Why are cooking and baking not hard work for mother? _____

_____

3. What do you think *tart* means? _____

_____

4. What does mother put in her apple pie? _____

_____

5. What does she put in the banana cream pie? _____

_____

6. Do you like pie? What are your favorite pies?

_____ _____

_____ _____

_____ _____

_____ _____

Fish Tank

Some people keep fish as a hobby. They keep the fish in a fish tank in their home. A good size for a fish tank is one that will hold 10 or 20 gallons of water. Fish tanks can be round, square or rectangular. Most fish tanks are made of glass.

Do not put a fish tank too close to a window. Too much sunlight through the window is not good for the water. Too much sunlight makes the water too warm. Small stones called gravel need to be in the bottom of the tank. A few plastic green plants in the tank are also nice. A fish tank also needs a pump that puts air into the water. A filter will help keep the water clean. A heater will keep the water just right—about 78°F.

1. How much water should a fish tank hold? _____

2. What is a perfect temperature for the water in the tank? _____

3. What can make the water in the tank too warm? _____

4. Where should you put the small stones? _____

5. Why is a filter important for the tank? _____

_____

6. Why do you think the tanks are made of glass? _____

_____

7. Choose a shape and draw a fish tank. Draw colorful fish and interesting plants in the tank.

Grama's Hobby

My grama has a hobby. That hobby keeps her very busy. She spends many hours enjoying her hobby. Grama's hobby is making clothes for dolls and teddy bears! She takes a piece of material and cuts out the shapes. She uses her needle and thread to sew. She sews the shapes together. She puts on buttons. She adds a little snap or zipper. Sometimes, she adds a tiny pocket.

When my grama comes to visit, she asks to see my doll. She asks to see my brother's teddy bear. Then she sews clothes for them that fit just right. She dresses them in her handmade clothing. The clothing is made by my grama's own hands! It is cute clothing for a doll or teddy bear!

1. Name six things that Grama uses for her hobby. _____

_____

2. Why does the little clothing fit so well? _____

_____

3. How much time does Grama spend on her hobby? _____

4. What steps does Grama follow to make the clothing? _____

_____

_____

5. What does *handmade* clothing mean? _____

_____

6. Who does Grama make her clothes for? _____

7. Do you have a doll or teddy bear? Write about it.

_____

_____

_____

_____

_____

_____

Natural Stuff

We have an aunt named Naomi. She loves to work with natural stuff. That is her hobby! Aunt Naomi picks up sticks from the yard. She gathers pinecones from a forest trail. She collects grapevines, and she saves flowers from the garden. Aunt Naomi even uses weeds. She keeps bags filled with natural stuff!

Aunt Naomi thinks and thinks. She uses her imagination! Then she begins to put her project together. She uses some of her pieces of natural stuff. She adds a colorful ribbon or a fluffy bow. When she is done, she has a natural form of art. She can hang her art on the wall!

1. What is Aunt Naomi's hobby? _____

2. What natural things does she collect? _____

_____

3. How does she finish her project? _____

4. Where are the places Aunt Naomi goes to gather natural stuff? _____

_____

5. Why is her imagination important? _____

_____

6. What can she do with her natural art project? _____

_____

7. What kinds of natural things do you like to gather?

_____

_____

_____

Writing as a Hobby

Sometimes children think that writing is work. When you write your homework lessons, that is true. However, writing can also be a wonderful hobby! Many people write just for fun! If you have free time, you might want to try writing. You can be free to express your ideas when you write.

Writing is a simple hobby to set up. Just get a pad of paper, and find a pen or pencil. Now you are ready! Try writing in your bedroom or at the kitchen table. Try writing in your front yard or on a park bench. Write your ideas freely! Write a poem or create a verse for a song. Write a letter to your grampa, or make up a story. Write about a pet, or express an idea. Just write!

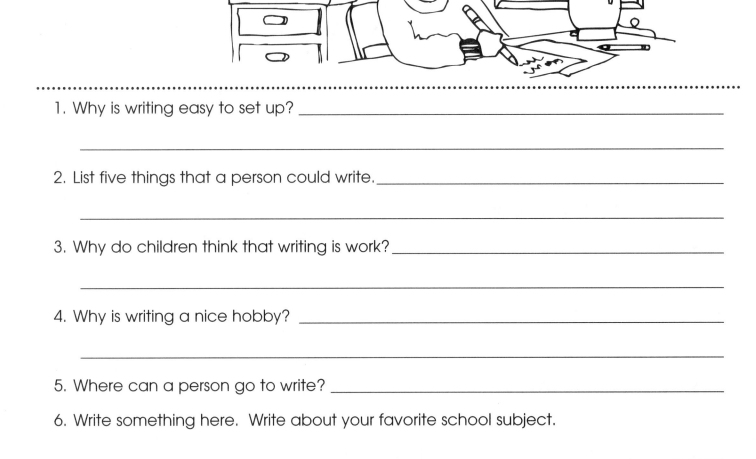

1. Why is writing easy to set up? _____

_____

2. List five things that a person could write. _____

_____

3. Why do children think that writing is work? _____

_____

4. Why is writing a nice hobby? _____

_____

5. Where can a person go to write? _____

6. Write something here. Write about your favorite school subject.

_____

_____

_____

Hands in the Clay Dough

My big sister knows how to make clay dough! She makes a big batch of clay dough in a pot. She cooks it slowly on the stove. When it gets thick enough, she stops cooking it. She lets me have it then! It is nice and warm when she gives it to me. That clay dough feels so good in my hands!

I squeeze the warm clay dough. I push it with both hands. I squish it down flat. Then I roll it back up! Playing with fresh clay dough is my favorite hobby! Sometimes, I make animal shapes with it. Once, I made a doll with my clay dough. I softly poked eyes into the doll's face. I carefully pinched a little nose on it. That doll was my best clay dough project!

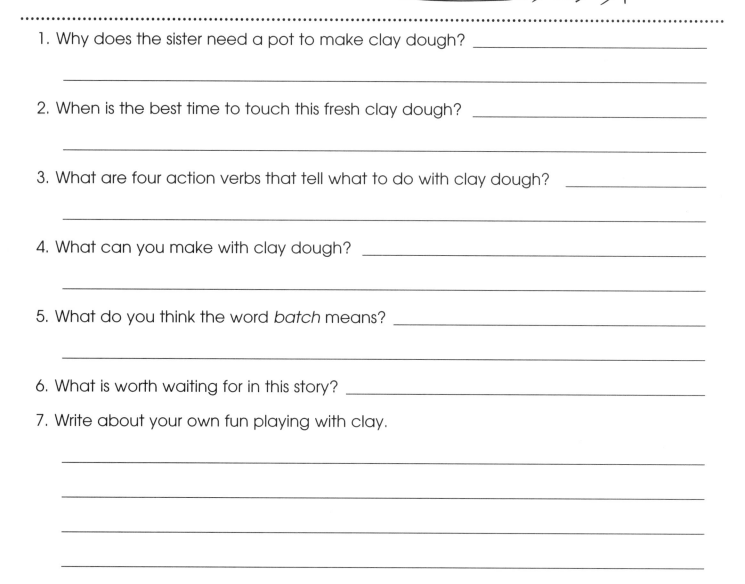

1. Why does the sister need a pot to make clay dough? _____

_____

2. When is the best time to touch this fresh clay dough? _____

_____

3. What are four action verbs that tell what to do with clay dough? _____

_____

4. What can you make with clay dough? _____

_____

5. What do you think the word *batch* means? _____

_____

6. What is worth waiting for in this story? _____

7. Write about your own fun playing with clay.

_____

_____

_____

_____

Birds Eat Bugs

People often think that bugs are pests. Birds do not think that. The bugs are not pests for birds. Birds love bugs! Birds eat bugs! In fact, birds control how many bugs are on the Earth. If the Earth did not have birds, there would be more bugs. Then the bugs would really be pests!

Birds hunt for bugs to eat. Birds find bugs in the air, in the dirt and in the grass. Birds also find bugs in the water, in trees and in flowers. Birds peck for bugs in the mud. They snatch bugs in the wind. Birds pull bugs right out of the ground! Birds fill up on bugs! They fill up their tummies with fresh, little bugs!

1. How do birds control the number of bugs? _____

_____

2. Name four action verbs that show what birds do with bugs. _____

_____

3. List nine places where birds find bugs. _____

_____

4. What do you think the word *pests* means? _____

_____

5. Why is a bug not a pest for a bird? _____

_____

6. From this story, why are birds so busy? _____

_____

7. Draw a picture of birds finding bugs in different places.

Growing a Garden

A backyard is an excellent place to grow a garden. All you need is a little space in the dirt. With just a little space, you can grow a vegetable called a radish. A radish is a small vegetable that can grow in a small space!

First, you will need to go to the store. At the store, you will buy radish seeds. Next, you need to prepare your garden. Use a spade to dig in the dirt. Make the dirt loose and soft. Then put the seeds in the dirt. Do not put the seeds in very deep. Finally, give some water to your garden. Then, wait for the rays of sun to shine and shine! Soon, you will have radishes to pull from the soil!

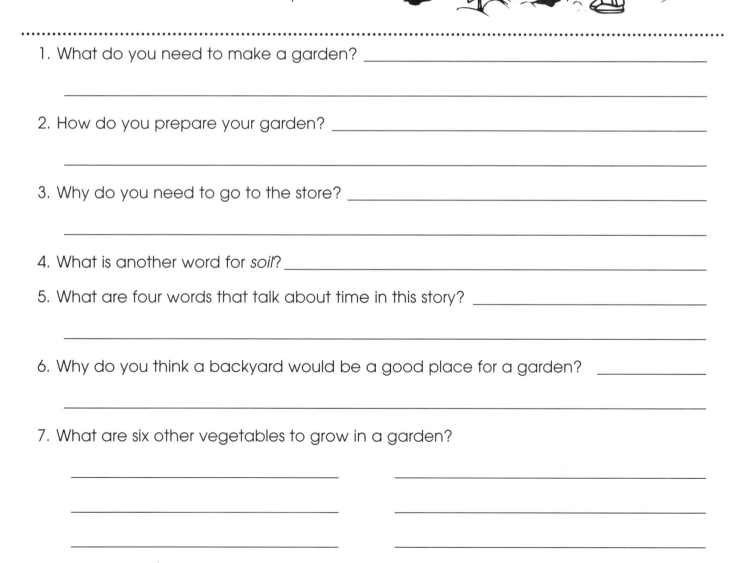

1. What do you need to make a garden? _____

_____

2. How do you prepare your garden? _____

_____

3. Why do you need to go to the store? _____

_____

4. What is another word for *soil*? _____

5. What are four words that talk about time in this story? _____

_____

6. Why do you think a backyard would be a good place for a garden? _____

_____

7. What are six other vegetables to grow in a garden?

_____   _____

_____   _____

_____   _____

My Backyard Bucket

I enjoy my backyard! It is not a large, fancy backyard. My backyard is just a small, simple place, but it is wonderful to me. I keep a shiny, tin bucket in my backyard. When the rain falls, the rainwater fills my bucket. My bucket of rainwater is one of my favorite things. I like to stay home and listen to the rain filling my bucket. Sometimes it rains when I am at school.

A rainy day at school
Is a long, long day for me.
I hear the raindrops falling
And I smile and laugh with glee.
My bucket will be filling
With the water from the sky.
I must wait 'til school is over,
Then I check to see how high
The water in my bucket is
So fresh and clean and cool.
For a tiny frog or turtle
It is better than a pool!

1. What words describe the bucket? _____

2. What word is the opposite of *simple*? _____

3. What do you think *glee* means? _____

_____

4. What word in the poem rhymes with *sky*? _____

_____

5. What besides a frog or turtle might enjoy the bucket of water?_____

6. Write down some ways to use a bucket of rainwater.

_____

_____

_____

_____

60

White Spider

The morning was bright and sunny. Jasmine opened her bedroom window to feel the fresh, cool air. The colorful curtain at her window rustled with the mild breeze. She took Mom's hand and said, "Let's go to the backyard and pick a lemon from our lemon tree!"

Jasmine went to open the door to the backyard. She and Mom stepped outside. Under the young lemon tree, they reached down to pick a soft, white flower. They both jumped back in surprise! A fat, white spider with eight, busy legs was running around the white flower! "White on white, light and bright!" they both smiled together. "Our natural world has many surprises," explained mom. Then they snapped a lemon from the branch above them. They laughed about the white spider. It had taken them by surprise!

1. What did Jasmine and her mom make a poem about? _____

2. Describe five things about the weather that day. _____

_____

3. What did Jasmine plan to do in the backyard? _____

_____

4. What didn't Jasmine plan to see in the backyard? _____

_____

5. How did they feel about finding the white spider? _____

_____

6. What words describe the flower? _____

7. Do you think they picked the flower? Tell why or why not.

_____

_____

_____

_____

Those Bees!

The boy chose a small, dump truck and a tough, little van to push through the sand. Then he said to Dad, "I'll be playing in the sandbox. I'll come back inside when I get hot and thirsty!" He shut the back door quietly. Then he settled down to make tire tracks in the sand. He used his small, dump truck and tough, little van.

He waved away a small bee that came buzzing too close to his play. Then he heard more bees buzzing. He looked up and noticed dozens of bees. They were moving in circles around the flowers on the apple tree in his backyard. All of those bees made quite a hum! Then he remembered what Dad had told him about bees. Those bees would pick up the pollen from the pretty, pink flowers. That pollen would help more apples grow!

1. Why did the boy take a truck and a van outside? _____

_____

2. Find six adjectives in this story. _____

_____

3. What were two sounds of the bees? _____

4. How long would the boy stay outside? _____

5. What grows on apple trees before the apples grow? _____

6. How did the boy use his truck and van? _____

_____

7. Write a short story about bees.

_____

_____

_____

_____

_____

Name _____

Butterfly

*Fly by, butterfly
Flutter by, flutter by!*

*The motion is quick—
On a leaf, on a stick!*

*The color is bright—
Orange, yellow and white!*

*The freedom is ease—
They fly where they please!*

*Fly by, butterfly
Flutter by, flutter by!*

1. How many times is the word *fly* used in the poem?_____

2. What do you think the word *flutter* means? _____

   _____

3. What does the word *ease* mean?_____

   _____

4. What word rhymes with *stick*?_____

5. Where can a butterfly fly? _____

6. What two lines repeat in the poem? _____

   _____

7. Explain what you like about butterflies.

   _____

   _____

   _____

   _____

   _____

Name _____

My Dirt Pile

I have a grand backyard! There are orange trees and apple trees in my backyard. There is an old plum tree that is fun to climb. There are roses that grow on a bush and grapes that grow on a vine. I love everything there, but my favorite thing in my backyard is my dirt pile! That is where I go after school!

My dirt pile is my world of adventure and fun! I keep two plastic shovels there and one strong spade. I keep a pie tin and a huge bucket there. I like to dig and fill. I like to pack the dirt down flat. I like to scoop the dirt and pile it up. Sometimes, I use my hands to dig and scoop. The dirt feels cool in my hands. My dirt pile is a good place for me!

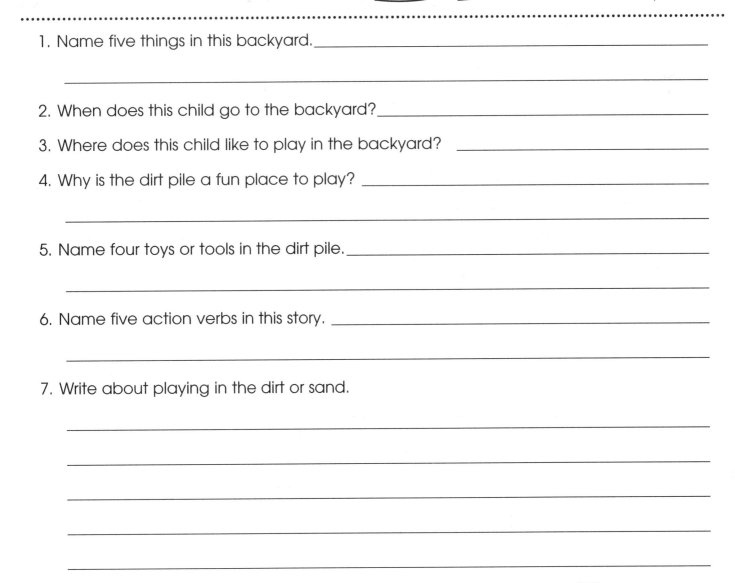

1. Name five things in this backyard. _____

_____

2. When does this child go to the backyard? _____

3. Where does this child like to play in the backyard? _____

4. Why is the dirt pile a fun place to play? _____

_____

5. Name four toys or tools in the dirt pile. _____

_____

6. Name five action verbs in this story. _____

_____

7. Write about playing in the dirt or sand.

_____

_____

_____

_____

_____

This Bug Is a Cricket

A cricket is a tiny bug. It is only about one inch long. It has two sets of wings, and it uses its wings to make music! A cricket rubs its wings together to make a musical sound! The sound is called a chirp.

A cricket likes to live in a warm place. Sometimes, a cricket lives inside a person's home. It finds a place to hide near a kitchen or fireplace. A cricket also lives outside in a field or a hole. The female cricket lays her eggs in a hole. She can lay 200 eggs in one year! The baby crickets that hatch do not have wings. The wings develop as the baby cricket grows up.

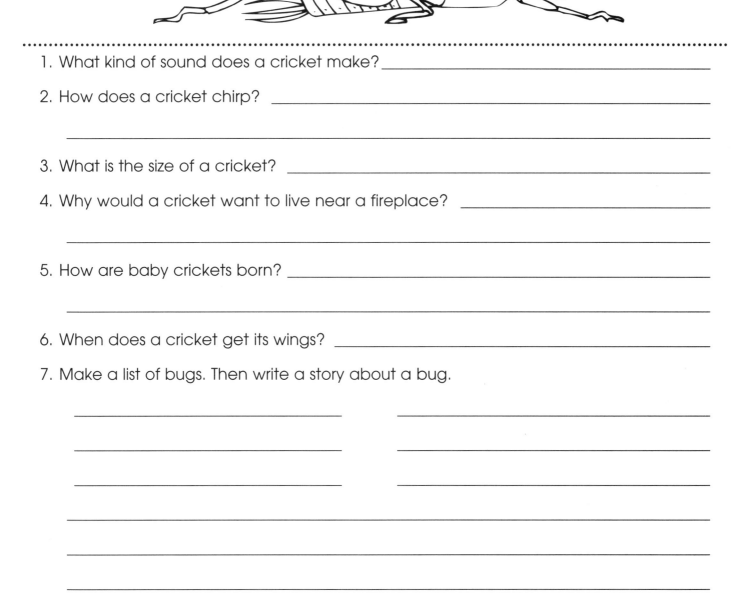

1. What kind of sound does a cricket make? _____

2. How does a cricket chirp? _____

   _____

3. What is the size of a cricket? _____

4. Why would a cricket want to live near a fireplace? _____

   _____

5. How are baby crickets born? _____

   _____

6. When does a cricket get its wings? _____

7. Make a list of bugs. Then write a story about a bug.

   _____   _____

   _____   _____

   _____   _____

   _____   _____

   _____   _____

The Empty Swing

Behind the house, an empty swing hangs in the backyard. The old, wooden seat of the swing is faded from many years of sun and rain. The chains that hold the empty swing are rusty. The rusty chains squeak and creak when the wind blows. The swing is empty because the children are older now. They look at the swing and remember.

The children remember swinging on autumn days with golden leaves floating down from the trees. They remember swinging on summer days with the blazing sun shining down. They remember soft snowflakes covering the swing in the winter. They remember raindrops splashing on the swing in the spring. The swing is empty now. But the children look in their backyard and remember.

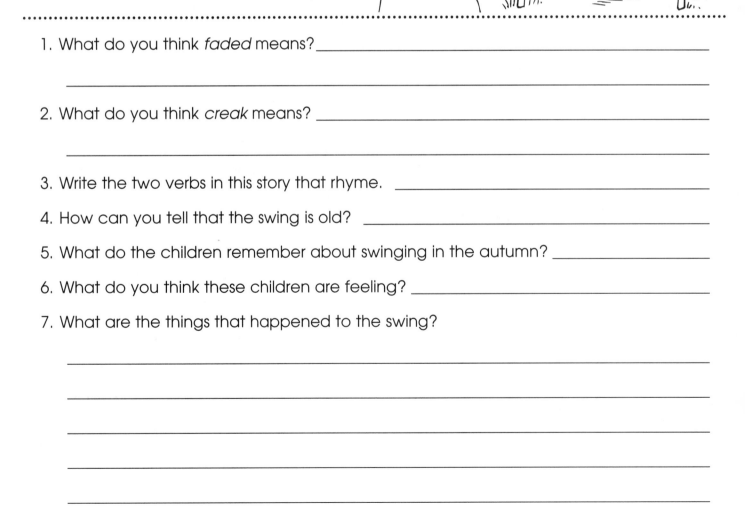

1. What do you think *faded* means? _____

_____

2. What do you think *creak* means? _____

_____

3. Write the two verbs in this story that rhyme. _____

4. How can you tell that the swing is old? _____

5. What do the children remember about swinging in the autumn? _____

6. What do you think these children are feeling? _____

7. What are the things that happened to the swing?

_____

_____

_____

_____

_____

TLC10425 Copyright © Teaching & Learning Company, Carthage, IL 62321-001

A Backyard Cookout

Carlos has an older brother named Pedro. Pedro is 21 years old. He goes to college in another city. When Pedro returns home from college, his family wants to celebrate. They celebrate with a backyard cookout. Pedro loves to cook! When the family has a backyard cookout, Pedro is the chef.

Pedro cooks beef on the grill. He puts pork ribs on the grill. Carlos loves to eat sweet corn. Pedro puts corn on the grill, too! The whole backyard is filled with good smells. Even the neighbors know that Pedro is home, cooking! For this family, a backyard cookout is a wonderful way to be together.

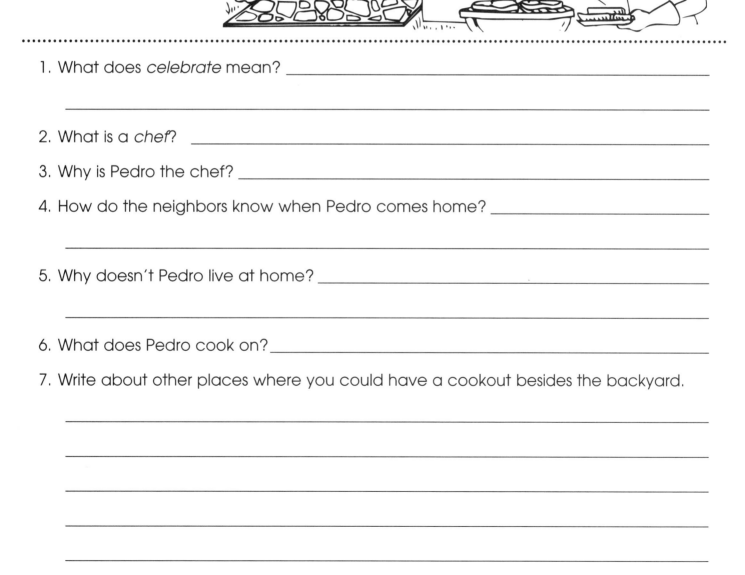

1. What does *celebrate* mean? _____

_____

2. What is a *chef*? _____

3. Why is Pedro the chef? _____

4. How do the neighbors know when Pedro comes home? _____

_____

5. Why doesn't Pedro live at home? _____

_____

6. What does Pedro cook on? _____

7. Write about other places where you could have a cookout besides the backyard.

_____

_____

_____

_____

Lunch for a Frog

Behind the old house, a frog lived in the shadow of a bush. The cats in the yard knew him well. The cats named him "Froggie." The cats were not afraid of Froggie, but they were very, very interested in him. Why were they so interested in Froggie? Froggie lunched on bugs!

Each day at lunchtime the cats watched Froggie. They watched Froggie catch bugs in the backyard. Froggie sometimes snatched black flies with his long tongue. Sometimes he munched on ladybugs. The cats watched Froggie, and they knew. They knew that bugs were a good lunch for a frog!

1. Where was the bush where Froggie lived? _____

2. When did the cats watch Froggie? _____

_____

3. Where did the cats watch Froggie? _____

4. How did Froggie catch flies? _____

_____

5. How did Froggie eat the ladybugs? _____

_____

6. Think of more bugs for a frog to eat. _____

_____

7. Find out how a frog is different from a toad.

_____

_____

_____

_____

Kitty Cat

A favorite house pet is a cat. A cat is very different from a dog. A cat can give itself a bath! It cleans itself with its tongue. A dog does not do that!

My neighbors have a cat;
They call her Milly Black.
Last week she had some kittens;
The cutest one is Jack.

We brought Jack home to our house;
We'll keep him as our pet.
We'll feed him, and we'll hold him
And take him to the vet.

So, now we have a kitty;
We have our little cat.
He's soft, and he is silky.
He is sleeping on the mat.

1. Why don't you need to bathe a cat? _____

2. Who is Milly Black? _____

3. Who is the kitten on the mat? _____

4. In this poem, how does it feel to touch Jack? _____

5. In this poem, what are three ways to take care of the pet? _____

   _____

6. In this poem, what word rhymes with *mat*? _____

7. Do you like cats? Why or why not?

   _____

   _____

   _____

   _____

The Watchdog

A watchdog is a dog that has a big bark. A watchdog barks to scare away trouble. In this way, a watchdog protects the family. Sometimes, however, a watchdog barks too much. Our watchdog does that! Our watchdog barks at a bird. He even barks at a gentle butterfly!

Our family has a watchdog;
His name is Mr. Sparks.
He watches out for trouble,
Then barks and barks and barks!

We know our dog protects us
At our home and at the parks,
But when he barks too often
We must silence Mr. Sparks!

1. What are the two jobs of a watchdog? _____

_____

2. When should a watchdog not bark? _____

3. Why shouldn't a watchdog bark at a butterfly? _____

_____

4. What two words in the poem rhyme with *Mr. Sparks*? _____

5. What do you think the word *silence* means? _____

_____

6. Write how you would keep a watchdog from barking too much.

_____

_____

_____

_____

_____

Momma Hen

My grama has a little farm. When my grampa died, my grama stayed on her little
farm. She says that she is not lonely. She has some cats and dogs, and she has
Momma Hen. My grama just loves Momma Hen! I think Grama talks to Momma
Hen. We know that Momma Hen talks back! Cluck, cluck, cluck, cluck!

Each morning on the little farm, Grama wakes up with a fresh start. She wakes up
with excitement for each new day. Grama opens her back door and goes to the barnyard. She goes out in her pajamas! She chats with Momma Hen, and she chooses a
fresh egg from Momma Hen's nest. Still in her pajamas, Grama cooks that one fresh
egg. She starts each day with one fresh egg from Momma Hen.

1. Why do you think Grama is not lonely? _____

_____

2. Why does Grama love Momma Hen? _____

3. Who used to live on the farm with Grama? _____

4. What does Grama wear to the barnyard?_____

5. Why does Grama have excitement for each new day? _____

_____

6. What do you think *chat* means? _____

_____

7. List other animals that might live in a barnyard.

_____   _____

_____   _____

_____   _____

_____   _____

_____   _____

My Parrot Is Not a Parakeet!

In the living room of my house, I have a cage. It is a strong and shiny cage. Inside the cage is my pet parrot. He is a large bird. He is not a parakeet! A person who has a parakeet has a small bird.

My parrot is a large bird;
His beak is called a bill.
He likes to have a warm cage;
He never likes a chill.

My parrot is a pretty bird;
His feathers are so bright.
My parrot is a strong bird;
My fingers he could bite.

My parrot is a smart bird;
He listens to me sing.
He hears my words, and then, surprise!
He sings the words I sing!

1. Where is the parrot's cage? _____

2. How is a parakeet different from a parrot? _____

_____

3. Why do you think the cage has to be strong? _____

_____

4. What words describe the parrot? _____

5. In the poem, what word rhymes with *chill*? _____

6. How do you know that a parrot is smart? _____

_____

7. What do you know about keeping a bird as a pet?

_____

_____

_____

_____

72

The Barnyard Pony

When I visit my friend Jenny, we always go out to the barnyard. We go to the barnyard to see Western, her pony. Western is an old, small pony. He is too old to give us a ride. Western moves slowly now, and his actions are gentle. When Western was young, though, he was quick and frisky!

When Western was young, he used to trot around the barnyard. Sometimes, if the gate was open, he would gallop across the field. He was frisky and full of action! Now, Western just takes it easy. The pigs and chickens in the barnyard are his friends, and he is gentle with them. When Jenny and I go to the barnyard, we go to see Western, the barnyard pony.

1. Why is Western a good name for a horse?_____

_____

2. How do Western's actions show that he is old? _____

_____

3. How was Western different when he was young? _____

_____

4. What do you think *take it easy* means? _____

_____

5. Find out what *frisky* means. _____

6. Who are Western's friends? _____

7. What do you know about ponies or horses?

_____

_____

_____

_____

Doctor Duck

The long, wooden fence goes around a large barnyard. The barnyard is large enough to have a pond. There is a family of ducks that lives at the pond most of the year. It is only in the winter that the ducks migrate south. There are 14 ducks at the pond, and one of them is Doctor Duck.

Doctor Duck is busier than the other ducks. Doctor Duck checks on each duck in the group each day. She checks their huge, webbed feet.

She checks their strong, yellow bills. She lifts and checks under their wings! Sometimes, when a duck is sick, that duck cannot say "Quack, Quack." That sick duck is very weak. The sound it makes is just "quick, quick." So, Doctor Duck takes care of the sick duck. She cares for the sick duck until it is well. That is the life of Doctor Duck!

1. In what three seasons do the ducks live at the pond? _____

_____

2. What four adjectives describe the ducks' feet and bills? _____

_____

3. What is the life of Doctor Duck? _____

4. How many of the ducks at the pond are not doctors? _____

5. How do you know if a duck is very weak? _____

_____

6. What two things does the fence surround? _____

_____

7. On a separate piece of paper draw a colorful picture of this barnyard scene.

A Pig for a Pet?

Most people do not think of a pig as a pet. Some people, however, do keep a pig in the house! A special kind of pig makes a good house pet. Usually, though, most pigs live in the barnyard. Most pigs are raised to be food for people to eat. If you eat bacon or ham, you are eating the meat of the pig. Sausage can also be made from the meat of a pig.

Farmers who keep a lot of pigs are called hog farmers. The farmers take special care of each little pig, called a piggy. Another name for a little pig is piglet. Maybe you know a famous character named Piglet. Then there is the mother pig. She is called a sow. There also is a wild pig. A wild pig is very dangerous. The word *boar* is used for a wild pig. A wild boar could not live in a barnyard. A wild boar could certainly not be a house pet!

1. What kind of meat from a pig do you like? _____

2. What is a mother pig called? _____

3. Why couldn't a wild boar live in a barnyard? _____

_____

4. Where can pigs live besides the barnyard? _____

_____

5. What are two words for *little pig*? _____

6. What do you think *hog* means? _____

_____

7. On a separate piece of paper draw a picture of a sow with her piglets. Draw a wild boar far away in the woods. Put tusks on the boar.

Fuzzy Bunny

A bunny is a young rabbit. It is fuzzy, and it feels soft to touch. A bunny is small, but it will grow larger. It will become heavier, too. The ears of a bunny will increase in size. Soon, it will look just like a rabbit!

A bunny seems to be playful. That is because it hops a lot. In fact, it almost bounces from place to place! A bunny likes to munch on crunchy things. A bunny has strong teeth to chomp on carrots and chunks of cabbage. A bunny's favorite meal is a salad!

1. What are three words in this story that mean "get bigger"? _____

_____

2. What two words tell how a bunny moves?_____

3. What five words in the story have the "ch" sound in them?_____

_____

4. What do you think *chomp* means? _____

_____

5. Why is a bunny soft to touch?_____

6. Why is it easy for a bunny to munch and chomp? _____

_____

7. Plan a big salad to feed a bunny. Write down five or six foods to put in the salad.

_____   _____

_____   _____

_____   _____

A Calf on the Farm

Sometimes a mother cow has a baby. That baby cow is called a calf. The mother cow is a mammal. The calf is a mammal, too. Because the calf is a mammal, it has some hair on its skin. Like other mammals, the calf drinks milk from its mother.

A calf usually is born on a farm. It grows up on a farm, too. It grazes on the grass. A calf has very strong feet. The foot of a calf is called a hoof. If the calf is male, it will grow up and become a bull. Any calf is also a bovine. *Bovine* means "cow."

1. What shows that a calf is a mammal? _____

_____

2. What do you think the word *grazes* means? _____

_____

3. Why is a calf also called a bovine? _____

_____

4. What is the calf's strong foot called? _____

5. Write a short story about a calf.

_____

_____

_____

_____

_____

_____

Goats in the Barnyard

Goats are interesting farm animals. They are very active and busy around the farm. They like to run and leap and play in the barnyard. They like to poke around the farmer's family. They often try to nibble on a person's clothing. Some farmers raise goats to milk them. Goat milk and goat cheese are delicious. Goat cheese is made from goat milk.

Not all goats live on farms. There are wild goats that live in the mountains, too. Almost all goats have little horns on their heads. They also have a little hairy beard on the chin. A few goats have fuzzy wool. However, many goats have rough hair.

1. Name five action verbs that tell what goats do. _____

_____

2. What do most goats have on their heads? _____

3. What do goats have on their chins? _____

4. What are two foods we get from a goat? _____

5. How are wild goats different from barnyard goats? _____

_____

6. What else do you know about goats?

_____

_____

_____

_____

_____

Space Science

In space, the closest object to the Earth is the moon. The moon actually belongs to the Earth! Does that surprise you? It is true! The moon travels with the Earth. The moon and the Earth travel together around the sun. It takes one year to do this. In one year the moon and the Earth completely orbit the sun. That is a very, very, long trip!

The moon is a ball like the Earth is a ball. However, the moon is very different from the Earth. The moon has no oceans or lakes, not even one small pond. The moon has nothing growing on it, nothing at all. The moon is completely bare of grass or trees. What is the moon? The moon is mostly rock!

1. What trip do the moon and Earth take together? _____

2. How long does this trip take? _____

3. What does the Earth have that is missing on the moon? _____

_____

4. What do you think *orbit* means? _____

_____

5. In what way is the moon like the Earth? _____

6. What is the moon made of? _____

7. Would you like to visit the moon? Why or why not?

_____

_____

_____

_____

_____

What Is Hail?

What is hail, and where does it come from? How does it form? Why does it fall? To find out this information, put on your thinking cap. Then read these facts about hail.

Hail is made from rain. Hail is made when rain freezes into little hard pieces. Because hail is frozen, it is very hard. That is why we can say "hailstones." The hard stones of hail are heavy. They are heavy enough to fall to the ground. Sometimes hail hits cars, houses and windows. Hail hurts if it hits a person. Hail cannot form in a clear, blue sky. However, on a cold and rainy day, watch out for hail! Hail might fall from the clouds.

1. How is hail different from rain? _____

_____

2. How is hail like a stone?_____

3. Why should you hurry inside if a hailstorm begins? _____

4. Why does hail fall from the sky? _____

_____

5. Why doesn't hail fall from a clear, blue sky? _____

_____

6. What does *put on your thinking cap* mean?_____

_____

7. Did you ever see hail on a stormy day? _____

Morning Fog

Frank's father fishes from a large, heavy boat. He fishes every day that he can. That is the way he earns a living. He fishes in the sun, and he fishes in the rain. The only time he doesn't fish is on a foggy morning. It is dangerous to take a boat out in the fog.

Each morning when Frank's father wakes up, he looks outside. If there is fog, he must stay home and wait. If the fog keeps Frank's father home, he turns his radio on. He listens to the weather channel, and he waits. Frank's father fishes in the wind. He fishes in the heat, and he fishes in the cold. On a foggy morning, however, his fishing has to wait.

1. What does *earn a living* mean? _____

_____

2. In this story, what does Frank's father wait for? _____

3. In what kinds of weather can he go fishing? _____

4. Why is a radio important to Frank's father? _____

_____

5. Why doesn't he take a boat out in the fog? _____

_____

6. What is the first thing Frank's father does each morning? _____

_____

7. What could Frank's father do to get ready for his work on a foggy morning until the fog clears?

_____

_____

_____

_____

Snowman on the Mountain

Gwen and Jamal were having a contest. They were watching out the car windows for the first flakes of snow. Whoever saw the snowflakes first would win! "It's snowing!" They shouted together. They both saw snowflakes touch the car window.

More and more snow was falling. Everything was beginning to look white. Father kept driving. Mother checked the map. The family was on their way to the mountains. They were going to the mountains just to play in the snow!

The snow became heavy. Father began to drive more slowly. Their car was going through the snow and up the mountain. Their car followed the curves of the mountain. They went around a big curve. Suddenly they saw a sign, "County Park." That is where they stopped the car. They all jumped out into the snow. Each person began to roll a big ball in the snow. They stacked the huge balls of snow to make a snowman. It was a wonderful snowman! It was their snowman on the mountain!

1. Why was the family going to the mountains? _____

2. How did the children spend their time in the car? _____

3. Why was County Park important in this story? _____

    _____

4. What was mother's job? _____

5. How was the weather changing? _____

    _____

6. For what two reasons did Father begin to drive more slowly? _____

    _____

7. Write what you like or do not like about snow.

    _____

    _____

    _____

    _____

A Breezy Day on the Bay

The children woke up first. They crawled out of their sleeping bags. The boat rocked back and forth. The family had been sleeping on their boat. They had spent the night in their boat on the bay.

"There's a good breeze blowing!" the children whispered to each other. "The sky is clear, and a breeze is blowing! It will be nice weather to sail our boat on the bay!"

The children smiled as Mom and Dad woke up. Mom got out the breakfast. It was in a bright, yellow picnic basket. Dad used his strong hands to raise the sails on the boat. Then he pulled up the anchor, and their beautiful boat began sailing in the breeze. They sailed all day in the breeze on the bay.

1. Where did the family wake up that morning? _____

2. What was nice about the weather that day? _____

_____

3. What words describe the picnic basket? _____

_____

4. Why did Dad need strong hands?_____

5. What do you think was in the picnic basket? _____

_____

6. List all the words in this story that begin with *b*.

_____   _____

_____   _____

_____   _____

_____   _____

A Strong Wind

People pay attention when the wind comes up. Even animals are aware when the wind picks up speed. A strong wind can mean danger. A strong wind can destroy buildings or blow down trees. Worst of all, a strong wind can bring a storm that hurts people. Sometimes a ship is lost at sea because of strong winds.

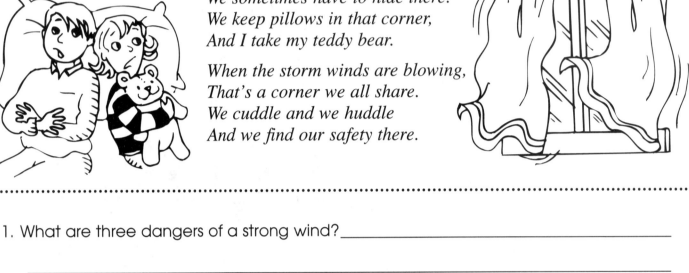

We have a corner in our house;
We sometimes have to hide there.
We keep pillows in that corner,
And I take my teddy bear.

When the storm winds are blowing,
That's a corner we all share.
We cuddle and we huddle
And we find our safety there.

1. What are three dangers of a strong wind?_____

_____

2. What do you think happens to a ship "lost at sea"? _____

_____

3. In the story, what makes people pay attention? _____

_____

4. What word rhymes with *bear* in the poem? _____

5. What do you think *huddle* means? _____

_____

6. How does the family feel safe? _____

7. How do you feel about strong winds?

_____

_____

_____

_____

What Are Liquids?

When you pour a glass of milk, you are pouring a liquid. If you have a soft drink, you are drinking a liquid. The water coming out of your faucet is a liquid, too. Even the juice from a lemon is a liquid. If you squeeze a piece of lemon, you get drops of liquid.

A liquid is different from a solid. A solid has a shape of its own. A liquid does not have a shape of its own. A liquid needs a container to hold it and give it a shape. Milk is a liquid. It can fill and take the shape of a glass. Milk can also fill and take the shape of a cup. What if you had a lot of milk? It could fill and take the shape of a bathtub! Imagine that!

1. What are three action verbs in this story? _____

_____

2. What are four examples of liquids in this story? _____

_____

3. How can you give shape to a liquid? _____

4. How is a solid different from a liquid? _____

_____

5. What is your favorite liquid? _____

6. List five more containers to hold liquids.

_____   _____

_____   _____

_____

Different Habitats

Our science teacher took us on a field trip. We visited three different places in one day! We went to the bay first. Then we went to a park near the canyon. The last place to visit was a baseball field! We were tired at the end of the day. It was a day to learn about animals and their habitats. It was exciting to do that!

There are so many different habitats for animals. That means there are many different places for them to live. We saw seagulls nesting on the shore when we went to the bay. Close to the canyon was the home of some deer. At the baseball field, our teacher showed us holes in the ground. He said, "That is where the moles burrow." Our teacher told us that habitats are very important in science.

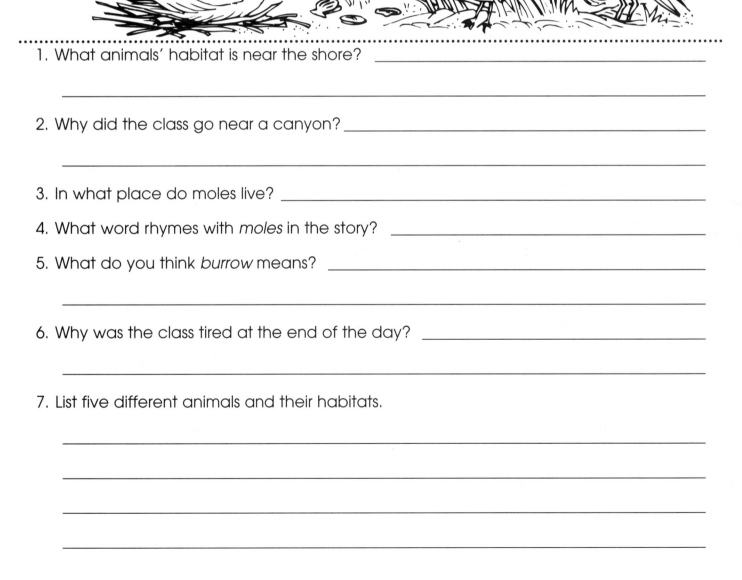

1. What animals' habitat is near the shore? _____

   _____

2. Why did the class go near a canyon? _____

   _____

3. In what place do moles live? _____

4. What word rhymes with *moles* in the story? _____

5. What do you think *burrow* means? _____

   _____

6. Why was the class tired at the end of the day? _____

   _____

7. List five different animals and their habitats.

   _____

   _____

   _____

   _____

Gentle Rain

The mother and her children woke up to a gentle rain. The children heard the rain first. They went quietly into Mother's room. Mother was just opening her eyes. "Is that a gentle rain I hear?" Mother asked her children. They all sat on Mother's bed and listened together. The rain was gently splashing on the windows. The rain was gently tapping on the roof.

"A gentle rain is a wonderful rain," Mother said to her children. "A gentle rain is not a storm," she explained. "There is no wind. There is no lightning. There will be no flood waters." The mother and her children enjoyed the sound of the soft and gentle rain. It was a peaceful sound, like good music.

1. Why do you think the children went quietly into Mother's room?

_____

2. Where did they all sit to listen to the rain? _____

3. What four things does a gentle rain not bring?_____

_____

4. What words describe the gentle rain? _____

5. Name two action verbs that tell what the gentle rain was doing. _____

_____

6. Write about why you do or do not like rain.

_____

_____

_____

_____

_____

Clouds

For many people, clouds in the sky are just something to look at. A person can lie on the grass and watch the clouds float by. A person can look up at the clouds and watch them change their shapes. A person can watch clouds form, and then paint a picture of them. A person can even look at clouds and imagine and dream. On a beautiful day, a person can relax by enjoying the clouds in the sky.

For other people, clouds in the sky are something to study and understand. A farmer studies the clouds in the sky. A pilot also studies the clouds. Even a sailor looks up to study the clouds. These people study the clouds to understand the weather. They know what kinds of clouds will bring rain. They understand what kinds of clouds will produce wind. They can tell what kind of clouds will create storms. The size and shape of clouds tell people about the weather.

1. What are five ways for people to enjoy clouds? _____

_____

2. Why do sailors need to study clouds? _____

_____

3. What three kinds of weather come from clouds in this story? _____

4. Why would a pilot check the clouds before he takes his plane up? _____

_____

5. How can a person understand the weather? _____

_____

6. Draw a colorful picture of clouds in the sky.

TLC10425 Copyright © Teaching & Learning Company, Carthage, IL 62321-0010

Nice, Spring Weather

The winter had been long and cold. People were waiting for spring to arrive. Day by day, the snow was melting away. Little streams of water were flowing where the snow had been. Now, the lake was free of ice. A warm breeze was blowing.

A butterfly fluttered across backyards and gardens. A mother robin made her nest. Green grass was sprouting everywhere. "Spring has sprung!" people shouted in joy. There was laughter! There were smiles! Spring was in the air!

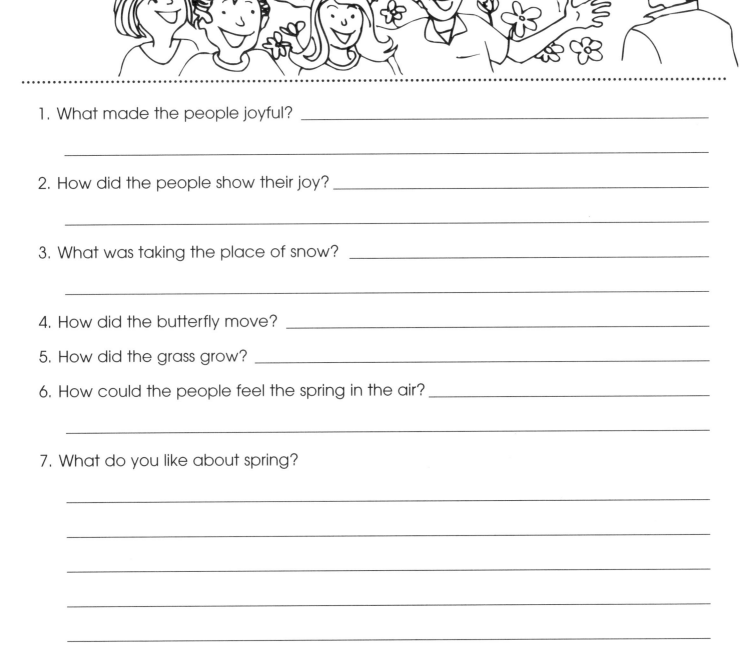

1. What made the people joyful? _____

_____

2. How did the people show their joy? _____

_____

3. What was taking the place of snow? _____

_____

4. How did the butterfly move? _____

5. How did the grass grow? _____

6. How could the people feel the spring in the air? _____

_____

7. What do you like about spring?

_____

_____

_____

_____

Hang Gliding

Sometimes my family takes a drive. We go to a high cliff above the ocean. We can park our car there on the cliff and watch something special. We watch people hang glide! They hang glide above the sea. They look like huge, strange birds in the air. They do not flap, though. They just glide and soar.

We think it must be hard to hang glide. We look at those people in the air. We think how brave they are, and strong, too! They have to be strong to hold that big frame on their back. The frame has wings on it. The people seem to hang there in the air. They drift with the wind.

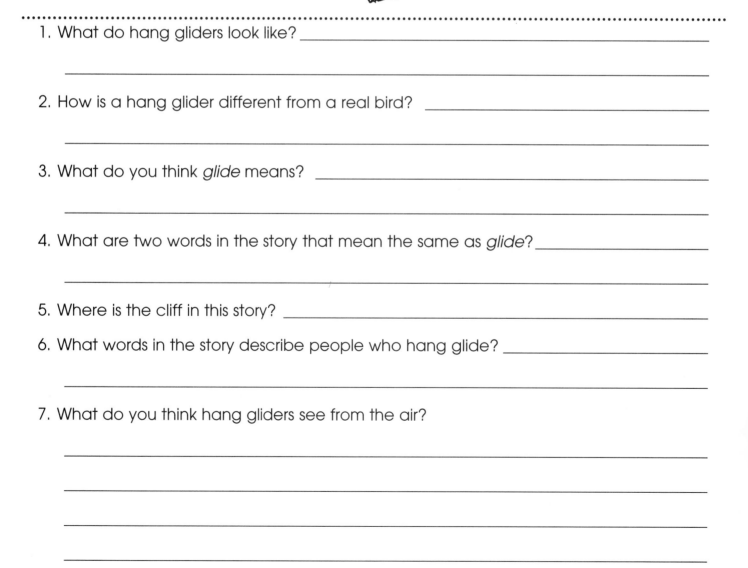

1. What do hang gliders look like? _____

_____

2. How is a hang glider different from a real bird? _____

_____

3. What do you think *glide* means? _____

_____

4. What are two words in the story that mean the same as *glide*? _____

_____

5. Where is the cliff in this story? _____

6. What words in the story describe people who hang glide? _____

_____

7. What do you think hang gliders see from the air?

_____

_____

_____

_____

Name _____

The Trolley

Sometimes my friend and I like to pretend. We sit on the long bench in my backyard. We pretend that the bench is a trolley. Uncle Todd put a little bell on the back of the bench. That shiny bell makes our trolley seem real.

We like to pack our trolley full. We put teddy bears and dolls on the bench. They can take a trolley ride, too! In the old days, a trolley went up and down the city streets on a track. People went to school and work on the trolley! They rang the bell when they wanted to get off the trolley.

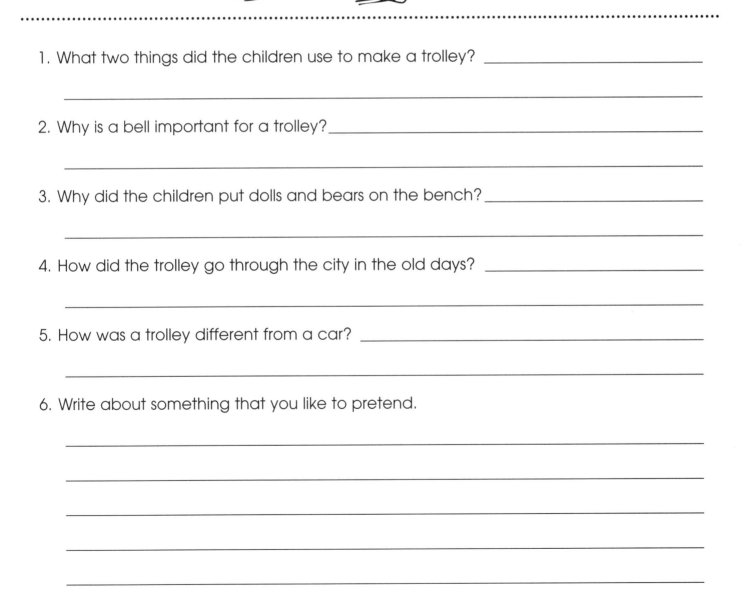

1. What two things did the children use to make a trolley? _____

_____

2. Why is a bell important for a trolley? _____

_____

3. Why did the children put dolls and bears on the bench? _____

_____

4. How did the trolley go through the city in the old days? _____

_____

5. How was a trolley different from a car? _____

_____

6. Write about something that you like to pretend.

_____

_____

_____

_____

My Family Uses Snowshoes

My family lives on the shore of a lake in a log cabin. We live very close to Canada. Our winters are long and cold! We have deep, deep snow for about six months each year. The snow makes it easy for us to get around, though. We walk on top of the snow in snowshoes!

First, we put our parkas and boots on. Then, we pull hats and gloves on. When we add our scarves, we are almost ready! We go out the door and put our snowshoes on. The snowshoes spread out our weight. We walk lightly on top of the snow! We can move quickly that way! It is a fun sport, but it is also a good way to get around.

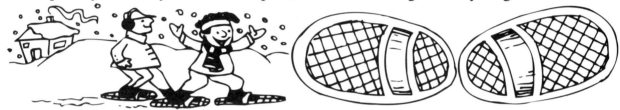

1. Where does this family live? _____

2. For how many months can they use snowshoes? _____

3. Why don't people sink down into the snow on snowshoes? _____

_____

4. What two words describe how they move on snowshoes? _____

_____

5. What five things do they put on to go outside? _____

_____

6. When do they put their snowshoes on? _____

7. Write about an activity you like to do in the snow.

_____

_____

_____

_____

_____

_____

On Foot

Do you know a great way to get somewhere? On foot! *On foot* means "by walking." Walking is a wonderful way to go someplace. Some people even walk on vacation! There are places in the world for you to do just that. It is called a walking tour. On a walking tour, people travel together in small groups. They walk together for many miles. They walk from town to town.

Walking is a healthy way to travel. When you walk, your heart is getting exercise. Your lungs fill up with fresh oxygen. This oxygen goes through your blood to your brain. That is healthy for your brain! People can walk almost anywhere—to school, to work, to play!

1. Where can a person go on foot? _____

2. Why do people take walking tours? _____

3. What carries fresh oxygen to the brain? _____

_____

4. What important part of your body gets exercise when you walk? _____

5. Why would a walking tour take a long time? _____

_____

6. Name four parts of the body from this story. _____

_____

7. Write about where you enjoy walking.

_____

_____

_____

_____

_____

Up to the Mountain Peak

Did you ever go to the very top of a mountain? A mountaintop is called a peak. There is a famous mountain peak in the state of Colorado. It is called Pikes Peak, and it is a very, very high point. Some people have climbed all the way up Pikes Peak. Other people have gone to Pikes Peak by bus. There is another way to get up there—by using the tram.

The tram to Pikes Peak is an exciting ride! After you buy your ticket, you get into a huge car. The huge car carries many people up to the top of the mountain. There is an electric cable that moves the car up to the peak. Many windows in the tram give people a large view of the mountain as they go up. The tram reaches Pikes Peak quickly, very quickly!

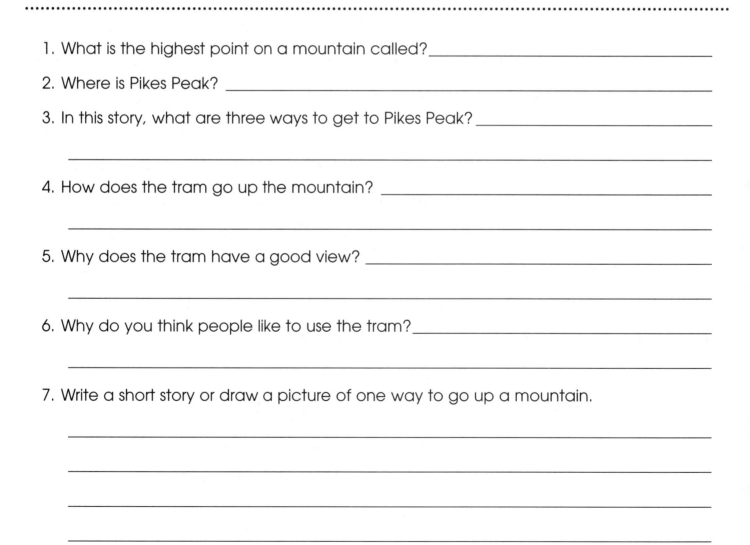

1. What is the highest point on a mountain called?_____

2. Where is Pikes Peak? _____

3. In this story, what are three ways to get to Pikes Peak? _____

   _____

4. How does the tram go up the mountain? _____

   _____

5. Why does the tram have a good view? _____

   _____

6. Why do you think people like to use the tram?_____

   _____

7. Write a short story or draw a picture of one way to go up a mountain.

   _____

   _____

   _____

   _____

Name _____

One Way to Get to School

Betty lived long ago, almost one hundred years ago. Betty lived on a farm with her parents. They raised corn and beans. It was a small but happy farm. They had just one wagon and one horse.

Betty rode the horse to school. It was a strong horse, but it was very gentle. The best part of Betty's day was riding her horse to and from school. They went slowly across the farm fields. Then they followed a dusty, dirt road. Finally, they went along the shore of a river to the school. The strong, gentle horse waited at school all day to take Betty back home when school was over.

1. How do you know that this farm was small? _____

_____

2. What else do you know about this farm? _____

_____

3. What two words describe Betty's horse? _____

4. Name three different places in this story. _____

_____

5. What do you think the horse did all day while it waited for Betty? _____

_____

6. What did Betty like about going to school? _____

_____

7. If you could choose any way to go to school, what would you choose?

_____

_____

Call It a Canoe

There is not just one kind of canoe. There are canoes of many shapes, sizes and materials. A person in the canoe uses both hands to control one long paddle. One person paddles a small canoe. A group of people paddle a large canoe.

Most canoes are long and thin. However, in one country, you can find round canoes! Most canoes are for one or two people to paddle. There are also huge canoes that 10 or 20 people paddle. Many canoes are made of wood or the bark of trees. Some other canoes are made from a whole, heavy tree log! All types of canoes offer a swift way to travel.

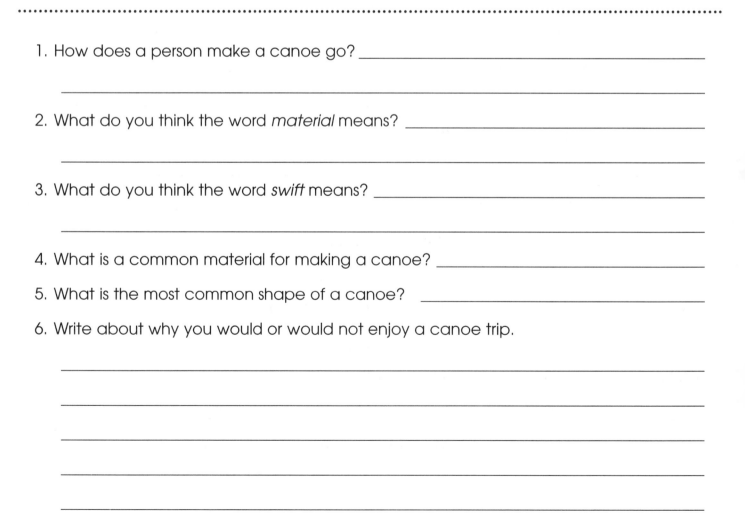

1. How does a person make a canoe go? _____

_____

2. What do you think the word *material* means? _____

_____

3. What do you think the word *swift* means? _____

_____

4. What is a common material for making a canoe? _____

5. What is the most common shape of a canoe? _____

6. Write about why you would or would not enjoy a canoe trip.

_____

_____

_____

_____

One Very Large Wagon

Father wanted to move West to new land. He wanted to travel and explore and discover something new. "But how will we get there?" worried Mother.

"Where will we settle down?" Jed and I cried together.

"Don't worry!" Father spoke strongly. "We need this new adventure!"

A few days later, Father and our neighbors finished building a heavy wagon made of wood. They put a huge cover like a round tent on top. They packed everything from our cabin inside the wagon. Father paid for strong animals to pull the wagon. It was a covered wagon, and we were pioneers moving West!

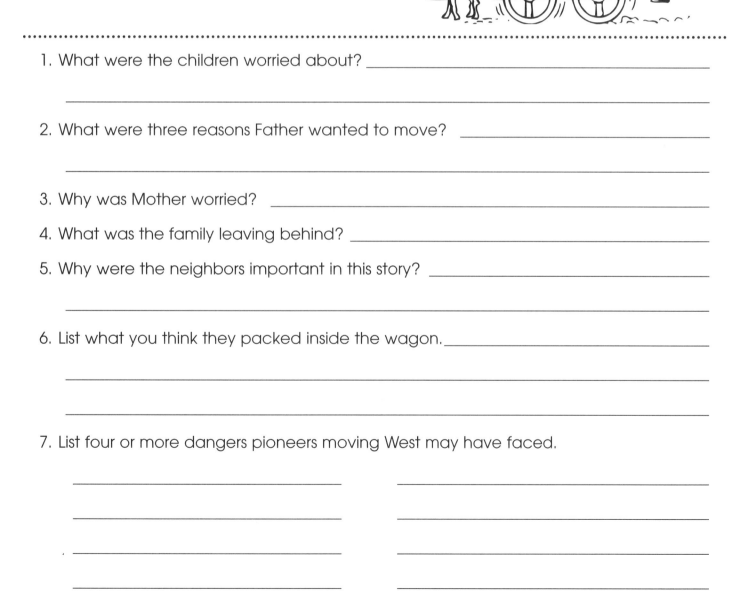

1. What were the children worried about? _____

_____

2. What were three reasons Father wanted to move? _____

_____

3. Why was Mother worried? _____

4. What was the family leaving behind? _____

5. Why were the neighbors important in this story? _____

_____

6. List what you think they packed inside the wagon. _____

_____

_____

7. List four or more dangers pioneers moving West may have faced.

_____   _____

_____   _____

_____   _____

_____   _____

Going by Bus

Going places by bus is a great way to travel! A person can go from state to state by bus. A person can go from city to city by bus. In a huge city, people often go from place to place by bus. Do children ever ride alone on a bus? Of course, they do! Children all over America ride on the school bus!

Dad puts me on the bus
When I am dressed for school.
I find a seat and settle down
And follow every rule.

Each day I have a long ride.
I try to never fuss.
My driver has a big job
To get us there by bus.

1. Where can you go by bus? _____

2. In the poem, what are some rules about riding a bus? _____

_____

3. Why is it important not to fuss on the bus? _____

_____

4. In the poem, what word rhymes with *rule*? _____

5. What line rhymes with *I try to never fuss*? _____

6. Do you ride a school bus? Why or why not?

_____

_____

_____

_____

_____

98

A Way to Cross the River

Ramon and I live with our Uncle Miguel across the river from our school. Sometimes Uncle Miguel takes us to school in the car. It is a long ride because we have to drive to the bridge. The bridge is not close to our house. The ride to school in the car takes almost one hour.

Our favorite way to get to school is not by car. It is by boat! Uncle Miguel has a wonderful motorboat. It is a racing boat and Uncle Miguel is a race boat driver. Sometimes he takes us to school in his racing boat! We do not race, though. We do not even go fast. We just cross the river that way. Uncle Miguel takes us carefully across the river. That is a fun way for us to get to school!

1. Why is the boat trip faster than the car trip? _____

   _____

2. When they go by car, how long is it? _____

3. What are the two names for Uncle Miguel's boat? _____

   _____

4. Why do you think the boat is their favorite way to go? _____

   _____

5. When do you think they might not use the boat? _____

   _____

6. Explain how you would like to travel to school.

   _____

   _____

   _____

   _____

   _____

A Poem of Hawaii

Hawaii is a group of islands. Hawaii is a state in the middle of the Pacific Ocean. Most of the islands of Hawaii are volcanoes. The bases of these volcanoes are under the ocean. The tops of the volcanoes are the islands!

*Hawaii is a state
In the middle of the sea.
There are many, many beaches
And the swimming there is free.*

*Hawaii has volcanoes;
Mauna Loa is just one
It pours out streams of lava
And erupts until it's done.*

1. Where are the islands of Hawaii? _____

2. What are these islands made from? _____

3. In the poem, what do you think *Mauna Loa* is? _____

   _____

4. What two action verbs tell what Mauna Loa does? _____

5. What comes out of a volcano? _____

6. What does *erupt* mean? _____

   _____

7. Draw a picture of volcanoes under the ocean. The tops of the volcanoes are the islands of Hawaii! Cover the islands with grass and flowers.

Mom's Dream

Mom has a dream. It is not her nighttime dream. Mom's dream is different. Her dream is her hope. It is what she hopes will come true. Mom's dream is to live in New York City! New York City is in the state of New York. New York City is one of the biggest cities in the world.

Mom likes the rush of traffic. She likes the noise of a crowd. She likes the busy feeling of streets filled with people. Mom likes the sound of a siren and the beep of a horn. She knows that the state of New York is not like that. However, she knows that New York City is just like that! That's why Mom's dream is to live there. To live in New York City is her hope!

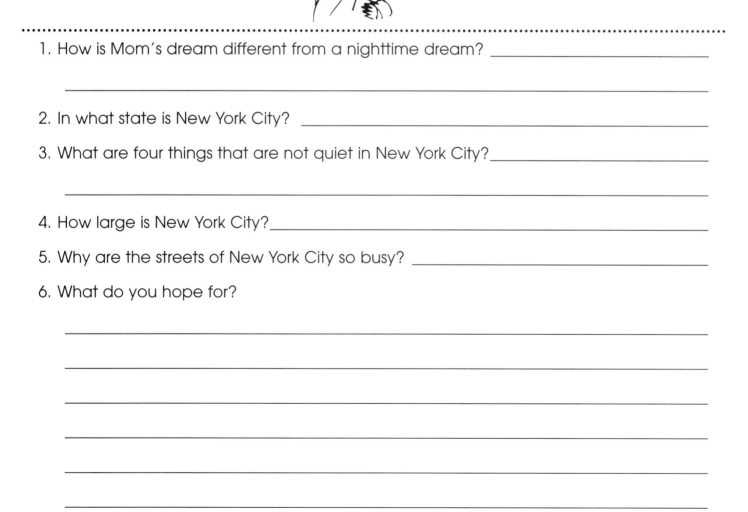

1. How is Mom's dream different from a nighttime dream? _____

_____

2. In what state is New York City? _____

3. What are four things that are not quiet in New York City?_____

_____

4. How large is New York City?_____

5. Why are the streets of New York City so busy? _____

6. What do you hope for?

_____

_____

_____

_____

_____

_____

Up North in Maine

Maine is close to Canada. It is a wonderful state with forests filled with trees. There are small mountains in Maine and beautiful lakes, too. The state of Maine also has seashores. The seashores are on the coast of the Atlantic Ocean.

Maine does not have long, hot summers. Instead, the summers are short and cool. There are not many storms, but the winters do have snow—a lot of snow! There is also plenty of rain during the year.

Wild animals are common in Maine. There are deer, and there are bears! There are many pheasants and wild ducks and geese. There are bobcats in the forests and seagulls at the shore. Maine is a very interesting place!

1. Where are the seashores of Maine? _____

2. What is the weather like in Maine? _____

3. What birds are found at Maine's shore? _____

_____

4. What other birds live in Maine? _____

_____

5. What word in this story is the opposite of *boring*? _____

6. Where do you think the deer and bears live in Maine? _____

7. Would you like to visit Maine? Why or why not?

_____

_____

_____

_____

_____

They Left Florida

My two cousins had to leave Florida. They had to move away to another state. They were quite upset about that! They did not want to leave Florida. They told me that Florida is their favorite state!

They told me many things about Florida. They said that where they lived, they could wear sandals all year, even in the winter! They told me about their orange trees. They picked their own oranges. They squeezed their own juice to drink! They could go to the ocean anytime. They could have a picnic on the beach in January! That's why my cousins will miss Florida, that wonderful state!

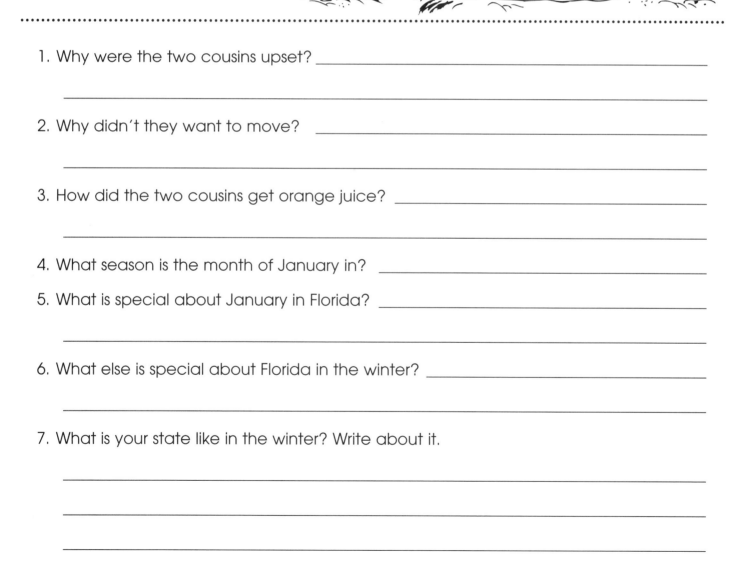

1. Why were the two cousins upset? _____

_____

2. Why didn't they want to move? _____

_____

3. How did the two cousins get orange juice? _____

_____

4. What season is the month of January in? _____

5. What is special about January in Florida? _____

_____

6. What else is special about Florida in the winter? _____

_____

7. What is your state like in the winter? Write about it.

_____

_____

_____

_____

Mike in Montana

Mike lives in the state of Montana. He has lived there for nine years, ever since he was born. The word *montana* comes from the Spanish. In Spanish they say montaña. *Montaña* means "mountain."

Montana is a huge state with mountains in the west. They are the Rocky Mountains, and they have great height. Mike lives high in the Rockies with his family. There is plenty of snow where he lives. There are many days when Mike cannot go to school in the winter. He cannot get to school because of the snow! In the spring the snow melts. Spring is when rivers are rushing in Montana!

....

1. What does the state of Montana's name mean? _____

2. In this story, what is another name for the Rocky Mountains? _____

_____

3. What part of Montana does Mike live in? _____

4. What does *great height* mean? _____

_____

5. How does winter snow cause problems for Mike? _____

_____

6. Why do the rivers rush in the spring? _____

_____

7. Would you like to live in Montana? Why or why not?

_____

_____

_____

_____

All About Arizona

One part of the U.S.A. is called the Southwest. A pretty state called Arizona is in the Southwest. Many people think of the desert when they think of Arizona. Arizona is not all desert, however. Arizona has mountains, lakes and rivers! Of course, there is something famous in Arizona, too. That famous thing is the Grand Canyon!

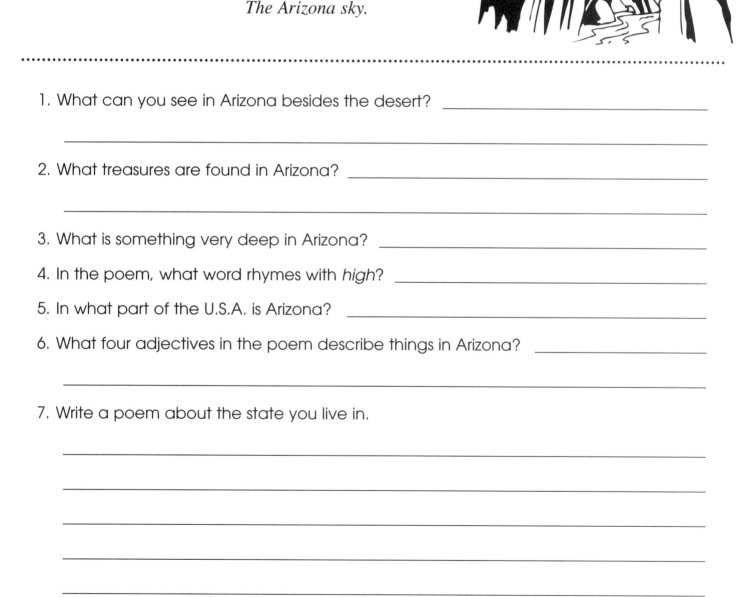

The deserts there are dry,
The canyons there are deep.
The gold and silver from the caves
Are treasures I can keep.

The rivers there are swift,
The mountains there are high.
The waters of the lakes reflect
The Arizona sky.

1. What can you see in Arizona besides the desert? _____

_____

2. What treasures are found in Arizona? _____

_____

3. What is something very deep in Arizona? _____

4. In the poem, what word rhymes with *high*? _____

5. In what part of the U.S.A. is Arizona? _____

6. What four adjectives in the poem describe things in Arizona? _____

_____

7. Write a poem about the state you live in.

_____

_____

_____

_____

_____

My Minnesota Life

I am a Minnesota girl. I was born in Minnesota, and I love my state. I live in northern Minnesota where all the lakes are. Did you know there are 10,000 lakes in Minnesota? My brother and I swim in the lakes near our town. We go fishing for little perch, there. We want to learn to water ski. Dad says when we are older we will get a ski boat! I can't wait for that!

Winter in Minnesota is very cold. Cold wind and air comes down from Canada. We still play out in the cold. We bundle up in heavy coats and boots. We make snowballs and snow forts, too. We do everything in the snow! We tramp in it; we slide in it; we even roll around in it. The most fun is to make a path for our sled in the snow. Minnesota is cold and snowy in winter, but we like it!

1. Why is swimming a popular activity in Minnesota? _____

2. What kind of fish do they catch? _____

3. What promise are these children waiting for? _____

4. Name four fun things to do in the snow. _____

    _____

5. Why does Minnesota have cold winters? _____

    _____

6. What do you think *bundle up* means?_____

    _____

7. Does your state get snow in the winter? Describe what you do on a snowy day.

    _____

    _____

    _____

    _____

Our Wisconsin Trip

Uncle Ben invited us to his house. Uncle Ben and his family live in Wisconsin. Their house is on the bank of a river. We had never been there before. We made our trip at Thanksgiving. There was snow on the hills and ice on the river. It was cold, so cold! Uncle Ben said, "It will be much colder at Christmas."

Uncle Ben showed us all around. He showed us the forest where he hunts deer. He showed us a big bay that is part of Lake Michigan. He explained about the ice on the river, too. Uncle Ben said, "The ice is not solid yet. It will freeze more. When it is frozen hard, we will skate on the river!" It was nice to visit Uncle Ben. We learned a lot about Wisconsin!

1. When did this family go to Wisconsin? _____

_____

2. Why is the forest important to Uncle Ben? _____

_____

3. How did Uncle Ben's place look at Thanksgiving? _____

_____

4. List four words that describe the season in the story. _____

_____

5. What do you think Uncle Ben's family is looking forward to? _____

_____

6. What else did you learn about Wisconsin? _____

_____

7. What is your favorite state in the U.S.A.? Explain why.

_____

_____

_____

_____

K for Kentucky

Kentucky is a very pretty state. There are many rivers in Kentucky and many state parks. There are mountains, too. However, the mountains in Kentucky are quite small. There are also many gentle hills. Here is something surprising. The grass in Kentucky is a beautiful shade of blue!

Kentucky has some areas of good farmland. Kentucky also has some very thick forests. In the forests, there are many different types of trees. Some of Kentucky's trees include oak, maple and wild cherry. Kentucky has plenty of rain. Wildflowers grow very well, and so do flowering bushes.

1. Name five things that make Kentucky pretty. _____

_____

2. What size are Kentucky's mountains? _____

3. Why do flowers grow well in Kentucky? _____

4. What do you think *thick forest* means? _____

_____

5. What do you think *gentle hills* means?_____

_____

6. What trees grow well in Kentucky? _____

7. Describe what grows in your state.

_____

_____

_____

_____

_____

_____

The State of Kansas

Kansas is in the central part of the U.S.A. Most of this state is flat and level. Kansas has a lot of great grassland for cows and horses to graze on. This kind of grassland is called pasture. Kansas also has huge farms where farmers grow wheat. Most of our breads and cereals come from wheat.

The weather in Kansas is not the best. Many summer days are over 100°F. Sometimes there is also a hot, summer wind that blows. In the winter, there might be blizzards of snow. In the spring, tornadoes sometimes form in the sky.

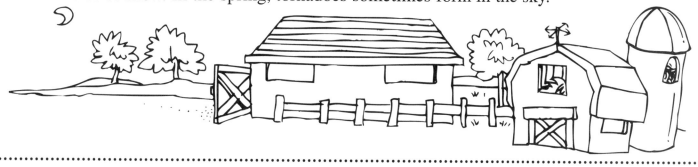

1. Why are the pastures in Kansas important? _____

_____

2. Why isn't Kansas near an ocean? _____

_____

3. What do you think the word *graze* means? _____

_____

4. What is important about Kansas for you and for me?_____

_____

5. Why are some summer days in Kansas not comfortable?_____

_____

6. What are two types of storms in Kansas? _____

7. What kind of bad weather does your state have?

_____

_____

Name _____

A Nice Place in the U.S.A.

New Mexico is a pretty state in the U.S.A. New Mexico is east of the state of Arizona. It is quite a dry state, but it has mountains that get plenty of snow. Many people travel to the mountains of New Mexico. They travel there to ski in the winter snow.

There is a small village high in the mountains of New Mexico. The village has an interesting name. The name of the village is Angel Fire. If you visit Angel Fire in the summer, it will be cool. In the winter it will be cold there. It will not be below zero, though. For that reason it is a wonderful place to go to ski!

1. How do you get to New Mexico from Arizona? _____

2. Why do people go to New Mexico in the winter? _____

_____

3. What is Angel Fire? _____

4. Why are the winters in Angel Fire cold? _____

_____

5. Why are the summers in Angel Fire cool? _____

_____

6. Would you like to visit Angel Fire? Why or why not?

_____

_____

_____

_____

_____

110

Read pages ___ to ___. Write five new words here.

Keep track of words you don't know. Look them up!

Look for these words in your reading.

I love to read! I have read these books.

Award Certificates

_____

has completed the

assignments and is an official

Reading Master!

_____ certifies that

_____

has some awesome

Reading Power!

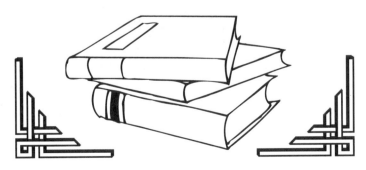

Super Reader Award

Presented to _____

by _____

Super Reader Certificate

Presented to _____

by _____

for outstanding work!